JUL - - 2000

You Can't
Catch Death

YOU CAN'T CATCH DEATH

A Daughter's Memoir

IANTHE BRAUTIGAN

ST. MARTIN'S PRESS · NEW YORK

Book design by Michelle McMillian

www.stmartins.com

ISBN 0-312-25296-X

First Edition: May 2000

10   9   8   7   6   5   4   3   2   1

To my daughter,
Elizabeth

Preface

*Fathers die. You keep on loving them in any way you can.
You can't hide him away in your heart.*
　　　　　　　　　　　　　　—MICHAEL ONDAATJE

We all have our roles in history. Mine is clouds.
　　　　　　　　　　　　　　—RICHARD BRAUTIGAN

My father was the author Richard Brautigan. He was born in 1935 in Tacoma, Washington, and grew up in the Pacific Northwest. He spent the early part of his childhood in poverty and was indelibly marked for the rest of his life by the Depression era. As a teenager he discovered poetry and made an outrageous career choice for someone of his social class: he decided to be a writer. This upset his mother; she wanted him to get a job. But the only vocations available for my father, who had spent all his spare time fishing, hunting, and doing odd jobs, were picking fruit and pumping gas. After a brief stint in the same mental institution where the movie *One Flew over the Cuckoo's Nest* was filmed, he left Oregon for San Francisco, breaking all ties with his family. He married Virginia Alder, my mother, and had me. In San Francisco he was influenced by the Beats and was mentored by the poet Jack Spicer. He became an original and subversive writer with extraordinary comic powers who loved the West. Richard Brautigan came into the public eye after *Trout Fishing in America* was published in 1967. The rest of his early books, *In Watermelon Sugar, The Pill Versus the Springhill Mine Disaster,* and *A Confederate General from Big Sur,* became fashionable with the counterculture movement. Catapulted overnight into an almost rock-star-like fame, he still maintained a work ethic that produced eleven novels, a book of short stories, and nine books of poetry.

In the early seventies he bought a small ranch in Montana and chose not to, in his words, write "Son of Trout Fishing in America" or "Grandson of Trout Fishing in America." Instead he wrote more Brautigan originals: *The Hawkline Monster, Willard and His Bowling Trophies, Sombrero Fallout,* and *Dreaming of Babylon.* In 1976 he also had begun living part of the year in the Kieo Plaza Hotel in Japan, which led to the publication of *June 30th, June 30th* and *The Tokyo–Montana Express.* Not a favorite with either critics or academics, he was nonetheless immensely popular with college students and was a significant influence on the literary scene, especially on the West Coast, although many critics never recognized him as anything other than a phenomenon. By the end of the seventies he had fallen out of public favor and his always heavy drinking got worse.

It might be tempting to think that his decline in popularity and his legendary relationship with alcohol were the reasons for his death, but you can't try to force a hypothesis. Just as the hapless detective C. Card, who is bewitched by a fantasy world in my father's novel *Dreaming of Babylon,* is left standing out of earshot of the solution to the mystery, so are we. For reasons that no one will ever really know, my father committed suicide in 1984. What I do know is that he led an extraordinary yet elusive life.

The prevailing sentiment when he died was that he was outdated and broken. Fortunately, the late Seymour Lawrence, his editor at Houghton Mifflin, made sure that most of his books remained in print. Popular in Europe, he is published in eleven countries, including Turkey and China, which I know would tickle his fancy. Since its publication several million copies of *Trout Fishing in America* have been sold. Instead of quietly fading away into oblivion after his death, his writing continues to be discovered by college students all over the world.

I started writing about my father because I needed a safe place to explore my feelings about him without having to explain anything to anyone. For a long time, I blamed myself for his suicide. I felt that if I had been a better daughter he would have lived. To make matters worse, everything that was written about him right after he died portrayed him incorrectly. Either friends wrote with old vendettas cutting sharply through their words, or journalists wrote without care or concern for who he was; their job was to write salacious stuff that would sell. I did not recognize the dignified, brilliant, hysterically funny, and sometimes difficult man who was my father in anything that they wrote.

My daughter, Elizabeth, was born a year after his death. I started therapy because I didn't want to be the gothic mother who never dealt with "the past," and I began to write down little pieces of what was happening to me concerning my father and his death. At first it was frustrating, because I wasn't getting it right. But one day I sat down and wrote a short essay, which I titled "Cannibal Carpenters." In this essay I was able to transcend the silence that suicide imposes, opening up a dialogue with myself and the past that ended up being this book. That day I realized that although my father was a public figure and would always be remembered in certain ways, I could express who my father was to *me* and the effect that his death had upon *me*.

For the past fourteen years I have led a kind of double life. On the outside I have tried to be a good parent, partner, sister, and friend. My husband and I bought an old house—which we still spend a great deal of our spare time working on—and I struggled with all the ordinary joy and despair that comes with day-to-day living. On the inside, all the while in a very quiet place, I was able to take my time and look around in the past and write down whatever I chose to about my father: how I remembered the corner of the living room where my father committed suicide or a conversation that he and I had about ballet. I earned an advanced degree at San Francisco State, sneaking parts of this book into writing workshops. I often wished over the years that I was compelled to write anything but this. One of his author friends, who I'm sure doesn't approve of memoirs, sighed and said, "You don't choose what you write." At times I questioned everything I was doing. How could all these little pieces add up to anything that even closely resembled a narrative? The writing itself was often dangerous. Unearthing the past does not come without a price. But slowly I began to realize that each piece was an antidote to a death/suicide that I was convinced on some level was infectious.

At first I thought I was writing to make him whole, trying to heal the split between the good father and the drinking father whom I had watched slowly become consumed by alcohol. And even though I was doing just that, I realized about halfway through the book that the very act of writing was forcing me to begin to live a life of my own choosing. Instead of remaining in the shadow of his suicide, I was dragging everything out into the light. I found myself doing things that I never would have done if I hadn't decided to write about my father's suicide; I took a trip to the Pacific Northwest to meet his mysterious mother, whose name he never uttered. In the end he remained just who he was, a very complex man whom I loved very much. It was I who changed, growing into a largesse of life that is my heritage.

Recently when I was showing my daughter some of the one-of-a-kind and beautiful writings and posters that my father had given me, she made two remarks. First she asked, "Can we keep all this stuff for generations?" I remember sitting back on my heels with everything I was showing her spread out on the living room floor and thinking some families have furniture and silverware; we have paper. Then she looked up at me and said, "Don't you ever want to run away and put the covers over your head?"

Elizabeth has been part of this journey as well. I tried to write the hardest parts with her out of the house, and I have mastered the art of answering her questions in a steady matter-of-fact voice. She deserves that and more.

This is not a book about therapy, nor is it a self-help tome about suicide or grief. I threw away all my books on both subjects long ago. Other than A. Alvarez's book and a short compassionate tract written by, of all people, a Baptist minister, most of what has been written on suicide was not helpful to me. I found that the writers wrote from an extraordinary distance from their subject, as if they were secretly afraid. Since I was already feeling so terribly alone and frightened, this was not what I needed.

Although I don't have any answers, I firmly believe there is no right or wrong way to navigate the suicide of a loved one, except to make sure you do. I don't pretend to be put back to rights. I just wanted to help break the silence that exists concerning suicide, so I broke mine. A serious fan of my father's sent me a letter after meeting me at a Beat conference. He wrote, "Watching you a bit and talking to you a bit has gone a long way in resolving, for me, part of the Brautigan mystery."

This writing is very private. It is not a biography of my father. He doesn't need to be explained. Everything that was important to him can be found within the pages of his books. And it is not a biography of me, nor is it a public summing-up of our relationship, or a celebrity tell-all. Instead it is a young woman's memoir about her own grief and what went on inside herself while she dealt with the mysteries of her father's life and suicide.

After I finished this book, I took a trip my father was supposed to take fourteen years ago. He was going to go to his ranch in Paradise Valley, Montana. He killed himself instead. After he died, I couldn't go to Montana. Although I returned on paper while writing this memoir, I felt sure that I would never be able to go back physically. I was afraid. But one beautiful fall morning, shortly after finishing this book, I received a letter from Lexi Cowan Marsh, an old Montana friend of mine. She had enclosed beautiful photographs of Paradise Valley and her many horses. The pictures made me realize that I needed to see the ranch. I bought a plane ticket and went. What had been previously impossible suddenly wasn't anymore.

After spending the night in Bozeman, I got in my rent-a-car and headed straight for the ranch. The Tastee-Freez we used to eat at was gone, and the creaky KOA campground's bridge had been replaced, but I had a feeling that if I went to Pine Creek at that moment, I would be able to get into the house and everything would be exactly the same. I was right. The ranch had just been sold, so not only was it unoccupied but the new owner, a kind man, let me walk into each room. There were still bullet holes in the kitchen wall, the results of an ancient drunken spree. Directly opposite I could see the pencil marks in my father's hand that recorded my height over the years. I never grew as tall as the bullet holes. I climbed up the flights of stairs in the barn to his writing room, still the color of a robin's egg, perched in the top of the barn. I looked out of fly-specked windows at the breathtaking view of the Absaroka Mountains. I left quickly because I had never liked his writing rooms. Later that day, I sat on the top step of the barn leaning up against the now locked door—the kind man with all the keys was gone—and I cried. Finally I was able to mourn my father without blaming myself for his death.

When the sun started to set, I stopped off at the Pine Creek Lodge and used the pay phone, staring out of the booth, mesmerized by a quality of light in Montana that only the painter Russell Chatham has been able to reproduce. I called Elizabeth and my husband, Paul. Elizabeth told me about her day at school, and Paul wished me luck. I drove up towards Mill Creek to my friend Lexi's. It was to her place, when I was fourteen, that my father had taken me to purchase my first horse.

After the second night of staying up late talking, first with Deane, Lexi's sister, and now with Lexi and her husband, Jim, I fell asleep to the sound of Mill Creek right outside my window. The next day Lexi drew me into the routine of her and her husband's life. We hauled cows down to PAYS, a huge auction house, in Billings. We went horseback riding up into the mountains. She was riding a mare who had been ridden only a couple of times, and I was riding the gentlest horse they had on hand, one of their stallions. I hadn't ridden since the fall of 1980, and I had never ridden a stallion before.

Later, on the hillside, the sound of creaking saddles and Lexi yelling at the mare, "Now, now, we'll have none of that," was familiar music to my ears. We saw a coyote, lots of mule deer, and a barn cat hunting, and checked on a bunch of cows in a high pasture. Just before we left, Lexi told me to have a good run. I galloped down the field, staying parallel to a stand of trees bordering an irrigation ditch. The leaves were bright yellow and the late-afternoon light was soft. I could hear Deane off in the distance urging me to take the chance and leave the ground beneath me, and so for a few moments the horse and I flew; I wasn't afraid.

It has been suggested by some that Montana hastened my father's death. At a reading a few years after his death a writer stated, when referring to Montana, "Wasn't that the place that Richard Brautigan went crazy?"

I have given thought to her words, but I don't think so. I think the beauty of everything kept him alive a bit longer, and I am grateful.

The last inscription he wrote for me, years before he died, reads: "This copy is for Ianthe, with love like a mountain range." I didn't fully understand the inscription until I had the courage to go back and feel the stunning impact of those mountains again, and only then could I finally accept my father's words into my heart.

What There Is Supposed to Be

There is supposed to be a beginning. One beginning might be the night I decided to let someone break into my father's house to see if there were any clues to where he might have gone. That night I dreamed about my father for the first time in my life. He was angry with me. "How dare you interfere with my privacy," he said to me in the gloom of the dream. An intensely private person about certain aspects of his life, he would not have allowed anyone in his house without permission. I knew how furious he was going to be with me when he came back from the trip he was on and found out. I still have the shiny red notebook that contains my incomplete jottings of that period of time before his body was found: "Dutch poet came to visit. Maybe? Amsterdam? Reed College? MOM." When I woke up the next morning, October 25, 1984, he was dead. A private detective told me this over the telephone. Realizing that I was slowly disconnecting from reality, I called my mother-in-law, the person who could reach me the soonest. The phone was still in my hand when she rushed into the bedroom where I still sat on the edge of the bed. I could see bits of what she had been doing before she came. Hair styled but no lipstick. Impeccably dressed but still wearing house slippers. I felt her arms slip around me, and she kept me from disappearing until my own mother arrived. A friend found my husband, Paul, and he came home. Then I stopped remembering for two or three or four days.

There is nothing to account for the lost time, except another dream. We were both in downtown Bolinas, California, and I saw his familiar long-legged figure walking fast down the narrow main street that leads out to the ocean. I ran to catch up with him. "Wait, Daddy, wait!" I called out to him. He stopped and looked at me for a moment, not unkindly or impatient or worried or angry. His blue eyes were filled with a kind of purpose and promise that I hadn't seen there since I was a young child.

"I've got to go," he said. "I have a lot of work to do."

I stopped running and stood still and watched him stride past Smilie's bar until I could see him no longer. Almost a week later, I finally felt beneath my bare feet the cold brick of the walkway in front of the little cottage where I lived. My mother was holding me in her arms and I was screaming. No one heard me because the neighbors had hired a rock band to perform at their Halloween party.

That night my unconscious and I made a bargain. In the daytime I would believe that my father was dead and would try to live that way, while at night I was released and free to dream about: a father who refused to die; a father I perilously loved almost more than my own life; a magical father who had begun to self-destruct, leaving me watching with no way to help him or protect myself.

Eleven years later, out of my new office window, I can see that the leaves are still mostly green on the trees in our backyard. The walnut trees are dropping walnuts, which the car wheels crush. The pumpkins are rotting on the front porch.

"Compost," my daughter, Elizabeth, says. She doesn't want to throw the bright orange pumpkins in the trash can. "We can cut them up and put them in the garden and they will become compost."

What was my father thinking? A friend of his remarked that he thought it was a failure of imagination: "If only he had stuck around, he would have dug on Elizabeth."

Another beginning might be his birth in Tacoma, Washington, and the existence of his mother and half-brothers and -sisters. He talked about his childhood in Oregon and Washington as I grew up, but no one was given a name. My father, who could create an entire imaginary world in his novel *In Watermelon Sugar*, refused to tell me his mother's name. He left Oregon shortly after he was released from the Salem Mental Hospital and that was that. He never spoke her name again.

The spring before I graduated from college, fragments from the past began to converge on me. I decided to try to write these bits of memory down and then maybe, I told myself, I might be able to find a place for my father and the effect his suicide has had on my life. I wasn't foolish enough to believe that I could trick death out of all its mysteries, but I did think that I was brave enough to bring back enough of the dead to go on living with less pain and more understanding than I had before. In my eagerness for a traditional narrative I opened the lid to the past, forgetting that the past is like Pandora's Box and is not easily closed once you have lifted the lid. And the problem with learning someone's name is that a name comes with a person and an entire life and yet another beginning.

This chaotic group of beginnings can't be ordered or categorized. This past is rich and huge and sprawls over everything. I'm learning that the more I let it take over, the more freedom I have. A part of me is terrified at what I'm trying to do while another is profoundly relieved.

In the middle of this kind of thinking, I go to the window in the living room to check on "the world's greatest sidewalk artists." What Elizabeth, my daughter, and Elizabeth Newman, one of her good friends, have created is quite startling, a half block of art. They started by writing their nicknames for each other, "Izzy" and "Izzy," followed by brightly colored fish, the same shape fish my father drew in his novel *Trout Fishing in America*. The fish float above sidewalk squares filled with rainbows with suns peeking through. Large peace signs dot the space. Right now, the Izzys are trying to trace the outlines of the brown leaves that are falling from the walnut trees. I can tell that this is not going well, the delicate leaves are crumbling. I leave the window, wondering what will be there when I go back to check on them. When I sit down at the computer I begin again.

In 1960, in San Francisco, our parents took pictures of Cadence and me at three months old. Cadence and I were born twenty-five days apart. She is the only friend I have that really knew my father. Cadence and her boyfriend have an apartment that overlooks North Beach. If you look out their bay windows, you can see Washington Square Park, where Cadence and I played together as children, and the preschool we both attended.

North Beach was my first world, the perfect-sized city-within-a-city for a child. Each block brought some new sensation. One

*Cadence and me in
San Francisco, 1960.*
© Virginia Aste

minute you could smell the sweet bread from an Italian bakery
and then the next the overwhelming clean of a Chinese laundry
or the sour smell of a bar at ten in the morning. The sidewalks
were kept immaculate by armies of old Italian women in house-
dresses and slippers. They sat on the stoops and chatted after
they swept with their old brooms. I skipped past them, staying
just within earshot of my father's shouts warning me to be careful. He worried that I might get hit by a car pulling out of one
of the many garages that lined the street.

Once, down by Fisherman's Wharf, I ventured ahead again.
Waiting for him at the street corner, I saw a small rat running
towards me. I knelt down and the rat jumped into my gently
cupped hands and bit me on the left forefinger when I stood up.
I still have a faint scar. A stranger threw her coat over the rat.
They were able to test the rat for rabies, and I only needed a
tetanus shot at the emergency room. My father had a long talk
with me about picking up rodents and told me a story about being bitten by a squirrel in Golden Gate Park.

"Why did he bite you?"

"I was giving him a peanut and he bit my finger instead of the nut." I looked for but never saw any squirrels in North Beach. The neighborhood literally gleamed in the daytime. No candy wrappers rattled against the curbs there.

If you went to Washington Square Park and played in the sandbox, there was a drinking fountain to wash your red, cold hands. The rich smell of cigar smoke floated from the park benches. The nuns from the Church of Saints Peter and Paul walked up and down the stairs that emptied out just across from the playground. When I was two, I thought they were penguins. Sometimes a wedding party would pour out of shiny black Cadillacs on the curb and glide upwards into the giant church that looked like a pastry to me.

At the center of the park is the Benjamin Franklin memorial. There are black-and-white pictures of my father holding me as a two-year-old in front of the same memorial. He is looking directly into the camera and at my mother, who is taking the photo. I'm happy. He is sad. He and my mother were within a year of splitting up. Five years later my father used the same memorial as the backdrop for the cover of *Trout Fishing in America*. I often wonder what that piece of marble meant to him. Why Benjamin Franklin? The easy-to-climb tree by the bus stop is gone, and now the park seems a little lonely there in the late afternoon.

From our apartment near the top of Lombard near Coit Tower I could watch Cadence trudging down the sidewalk from the direction of Sarah B. Cooper Elementary School on the other side of Columbus Avenue. We were both in the second grade, except I had just come back from Mexico with my mother and wasn't enrolled in school.

Instead I hung out the bay window and waited until Cadence got right below me and tried to spit on her from the second story.

My father picked me up at that same apartment. He came from the same direction Cadence did. I was so happy to see him walking up the hill towards me. I just barely endured the times when my mother took me away from San Francisco and thus my father. For a good many years after they split up, my mother and I moved around the Bay Area a great deal. And once my mother finally began to settle down, my father began moving. But for most of my childhood he rarely left San Francisco, so he and that city will be forever linked in my mind.

My father and me in Washington Square Park, San Francisco, at the Benjamin Franklin Memorial, 1962. © Virginia Aste

Sometimes he took me to the park and sat near me and watched me play. I liked to be pushed endlessly on the swings. There was an ice cream store on the same side of the square the church was on. If I was extremely lucky, he would buy me an ice cream. Although I didn't know it then, we were poor. Some time later, the ice cream place became Mama's Restaurant. And suddenly he was famous and had the money to buy me lunch there. He let me order whatever I wanted. The walls were white. The owner said hi to us. I could only shyly wave at her.

Other times we caught the bus from an island in the middle of Columbus Avenue right across from Washington Square Park. There is a tiny park at that bus stop. It has a bronze statue of a man looking into a little pond. An iron fence guards the miniature garden inside. No one is allowed to go in. I always wished I could, but instead I held on to my father's soft, warm hand and got on the bus.

A few years after my father died, I went to San Francisco on my birthday and sat on the edge of the sandbox in Washington Square Park and watched the children play. I touched the cold white-and-black-flecked marble of the Benjamin Franklin memorial and felt only silence. I wandered throughout North Beach, going down to Broadway past what used to be the famous Vanessi's restaurant, where many nights I had fallen asleep in a booth long before the party was over. Just down the block was Enrico's, a sidewalk café where my father and I spent hours and hours. My father would visit with friends and even an enamored stranger or two, while I read comics and ate coffee ice cream. The City Lights Bookstore gave me a jolt. It was exactly the same as I remembered it as a twenty-one-year-old woman, a seventeen-year-old girl, and a four-year-old child. Only now my tall, lanky father was not with me.

Late at night after my father's wake at Enrico's, my husband, Cadence, and I drove past the location of his old Geary Street apartment. I knew that the building had been torn down a long time ago, but the red neon light of the little caboose drive-in on the corner still blinked at me through the fog. The nearest bus stop is in front of the building that used to be a huge Sears department store. I didn't like that bus stop because the wind blew there all the time and my legs were always cold.

The two Elizabeths are still drawing. They gave up trying to trace leaves and have now begun drawing a large tree that grows horizontally from the rest of their work. This time the two girls see me and wave at me with their chalk-colored fingers. When I pass the window again, the girls are finishing drawing a large horse. I let the walls of time collapse and venture back into the year 1966 and into my father's Geary Street apartment in San Francisco. For a long time, nine years or so, that apartment kept my father safe.

Geary Street

When I was five my father moved into the apartment out on Geary Street. If you turn off Van Ness and go down Geary in the direction of the ocean you will see a large BEKINS sign at the top of the hill across from what used to be Sears. Don't go through the underpass, instead stay to the right, and you will pass the red caboose drive-in. Slow down and keep your eyes fixed on the new condominiums. His place used to be right there in the middle of the block. The building was a typical turn-of-the-century San Francisco apartment building. At the top of a set of stairs were two doors. If you went through my father's door you ended up inside a funny-shaped hallway with lots of other doors. His apartment door had a small window, and my father had taped some interesting things against the glass. There was a Digger dollar and a feather. For a while in the sixties the Diggers tried to present an alternative to capitalism. They opened a Free Store and created Digger dollars. They packed tables full of food under the eucalyptus trees in Golden Gate Park, and my father had taken me there to eat with them.

I quit sucking my thumb cold turkey in that apartment. Both Cadence and I were big thumb-suckers. One night, when I was six years old, my father and I were standing in the hallway. He watched me for a moment or two and said, "Aren't you a little old to be sucking your thumb?" I tilted my head up, having to squint slightly because of the harsh glare of the bare light-bulb; I instantly removed my slightly wrinkled thumb from my mouth and never put it there again.

Until I was about ten, getting to his apartment was easy. When I lived in the city, which was on and off from the time when I was born until just before I turned nine, he just picked me up in the afternoon from wherever I was living and we took the city bus together. Then my mother and I, and by now two sisters, Ellen and Mara, moved to Sonoma County. My brother, Jesse, would be born within the year. I began making the sixty-mile trip to San Francisco on the Greyhound bus. A round-trip ticket cost $4.10. I still have the carbon of a used ticket. For a while he picked me up at the old Greyhound station on Seventh Street in San Francisco. After I turned ten, he instructed me how to take a taxi to his place; I would give the driver the address and tell him to wait while I ran upstairs to get my father and he would pay the fare.

I wasn't afraid to hail a cab, because there was always a line of them at the curb. Nor did navigating the odd collection of people at the bus station frighten me. Instead I was always worried that there would be some sort of mix-up and he wouldn't be at home. Leaning forward anxiously, my chin resting on the divider between the front and back seats, I guided the cabby until we were right in the front of the apartment building. I would leave my bag and run up the stairs to the big door on the right. It was a heavy ornate carved wooden door so old that grime and dirt were caked sixty years thick in the crevices of the carvings. The buzzer had broken in about 1968, forcing me to bang as hard as I could. Afraid, the wind blowing at my back, I stood with my knuckles stinging, hoping that he would be able to hear my knock. He always did.

I much preferred it when he met me at the bus station. "You used to need a ticket to sleep at the bus station," he said absent-mindedly one day as we were walking past the ticket sellers' booths. I wasn't really paying attention to what he said. There were always people sleeping in this station with their belongings tucked around their feet. Instead I was on the lookout for the enormous dark-haired man who worked there. I liked watching the ticket seller give change. Dimes and nickels became miniaturized in the palms of his giant-sized hands. I looked up at my father in surprise when his words sank in and realized with a shock that he must have tried to sleep in bus stations and had gotten kicked out because he didn't have a ticket. I held tight to his hand at that moment, wishing that I could see what he was seeing with his worried blue eyes. His fingers were long and delicate, not anything like the giant man's. I gripped them tighter, but he didn't notice. He was looking off into space just a couple of feet above my head. Then my father shifted his gaze to look down at me, and we were standing together again on the battered linoleum floor in the middle of the bus station.

As a child I always liked that my father was instantly recogniz-able. There was never any doubt who he was, standing tall and slightly hunched at the shoulder with flyaway wavy, golden hair, his body twisted in a striking pose, not resembling, in the slightest, anyone else around him. Just the sight of him was tremendously reassuring for me.

My father standing on Geary Street, 1971.
© Ianthe Brautigan Swensen

Another benefit when my father met me at the bus station was I had his full attention. We would venture over toward Union Square and have lunch at a red-wallpapered Tad's Steak House on O'Farrell. This was back when downtown San Francisco had an odd, empty air about it. A lot of the shops on Market Street were closed and the windows were covered with newspapers or whitewash. We never went into Union Square. We never took a cable car. My desire was so strong to ride a cable car with him that I asked repeatedly over the years.

"You haven't seen what happens when a car runs a light and hits a cable car. It's a real horror show."

"Please."

"Severed legs."

"Just once."

"Amputated arms."

"But look at all those people—they don't seem worried."

"Crazy tourists."

His reaction was always the same. Predictable. When I got to be a teenager, I continued to ask just to watch him recreate carnage and mayhem in the middle of an ordinary foggy San Francisco afternoon.

When the door opened at the Geary Street apartment and my father appeared, he was usually distracted. Sometimes he was on the phone, sometimes we just had to hurry up to go on to another destination to meet friends or one of his girlfriends, or to complete business such as mailing off a manuscript. He never hired a baby-sitter when I stayed with him. Rarely would he just stop what he was doing and say hello. Thinking about this now, I suspect his mood had to do with becoming famous very fast. Between 1967 and 1968 my father published two novels and two books of poetry and also released a record album of him reading his work. Now, instead of carefully considering whether he could afford the fifteen cents for bus fare, his pockets were filled with wadded-up dollar bills. He didn't talk to me about what was happening. Dealing with the attention and responsibilities that his new fame brought must have been overwhelming. I just knew that sometimes he was irritable in a way that he had never been before. So for a while it was the apartment that greeted me with its soothing smells: an odd mixture of dust, just plain oldness, paper, and the tangy scent of metal.

There were faded fish painted on the floor leading down a long hallway, and a strange little antique phone that used to work inset in the wall. He would drop my overnight bag into his writing room, which I felt was haunted, while I slowly trailed behind. When he was in a hurry, my only connection to the apartment was using the bathroom, which contained a Beatles poster I especially liked.

The frosted glass in the bathroom door had a bumpy texture that was interesting to look at, as was a small leaflet thumb-tacked to the wall that I had memorized. "Color the picture, remember the rules, turn down gifts from strangers, avoid dark and lonely streets, know your local policeman."

Usually I had time to look around, because he would be on the phone. If this was the case I wandered, carefully touching my favorite things.

A curiously dust-free built-in bookshelf contained the bulk of his collection, all of which I was free to handle. A card saying "You have been assisted by a member of the Hell's Angels" was intriguing, as was the switchblade in the shape of a dragon, which was stuck open and wrapped in a rosary. A jar of pears, or maybe peaches, sat glimmering in a corner for years. A mink cover to a small Bible was comforting against my cheek. A small piece of gold lamé that Janis Joplin had given him was curiously heavier than it looked.

Sometimes I would find a new addition to the collection. When I was just at the right age, eleven, I found a box of chocolate-covered insects, which I begged to take home. He told me I could take them and even feed them to my unknowing friends, which was exactly what I wanted to do, on the condition that I eat one first. (He had a strict code of justice.) Of course I wouldn't, so they stayed.

A long, quiet afternoon was spent reading William Goldman's screenplay for *Butch Cassidy and the Sundance Kid.* The script had a place of honor on a stepladder that the well-known artist Bruce Connor had painted black and decorated with little pink pompoms hanging down on each step. Over by the fireplace that never worked was an old car horn that I liked to toot. In one corner of that room sat his fishing pole. I had caught a small rain-bow trout with a salmon egg when I was six while sitting on a sun-warmed rock by a bridge with him. So I didn't mind that he was always reminding me not to knock the pole over.

For a period of time his brass bed was covered with a buffalo hide I liked to press my face against. His bed was always made and in the middle of the buffalo hide was my father's idea of a Buddhist shrine: a bowl with a few quartz rocks he found while fishing and a couple of faded bus transfers. The sun shone in the window by his bed, gently fading anything that he placed in its way. The kitchen was small, with linoleum so old that there were big patches with no color at all. Under a dusty window was a stained porcelain sink with an old-fashioned spigot. A white fridge which never had much in it stood in the corner. The art on the wall included interesting things, like a pencil drawing of a bus with real Lincoln penny heads as passengers, a few small Fillmore Auditorium posters, and a picture of an ancient Colt pistol. The round oak table was ancient-looking with the stained rings of coffee cups. These left evidence of long conversations with his friends along with the black burnt half-circle of a pan put on the table. A couple of chairs with only a skeleton of ragged caning left in the seats, never neatly pushed in to the table, completed the picture. When I was really little, these chairs were problematic. I had to be careful how I got up or sat down because I feared I could be swallowed up in the places where the caning was missing on the seat.

The back porch was terrifying, piled almost up to the ceiling with many years' worth of the *San Francisco Chronicle.* He read the paper every day and then it would join the stack on the back porch. I don't know why he didn't throw them away. Sometimes I would attempt to go to the backyard, squeezing past the towers of newspapers, holding tightly to the railing of the rickety stairway to the dark ivy-colored expanse below.

My father had a running battle with the cats that liked to

howl on the back fence in the middle of the night. I looked long and hard for those cats but never saw or even heard one. But I do have the alarm clock that stopped working after he had thrown it at them in the middle of the night. The clock looks like a large black Chiclet, except it has art deco green numbers and a silver-plated back. It sat for years on the windowsill by his bed. I liked to wind it up for him.

"Not too tight or you'll break it," he warned me. After all those years of telling me to be careful, he threw the clock out the window.

Unlike the fridge, his kitchen cupboard contained things to eat: canned chili, sardines, and instant coffee. He had a small set of white tin dishes which had pictures of fruit on them. Sometimes he would open up a can of sardines and put them on a plate. I liked looking at the little fish almost as much as I liked eating them.

My father always had very clean hands. It seemed to me he held a kind of vigilance over his hands, every so often holding them up to careful inspection, looking at his fingers and then turning his hands over and looking at his palms and then flipping them back over with a Mary Poppins kind of satisfaction at their immaculateness. So hand washing preceded a lot of things I wanted to do in his apartment—touching any kind of paper, typing—and then there was the arriving and departing washing of hands. I must have driven him crazy with my grubby fingers, but he never let me know. He was just the father who washed his hands with big bars of white soap and sent me off to the bathroom to do the same. Sometimes to save time, because I could easily get distracted on the way to the bathroom that the sink was in, he just sent me to the kitchen, and I washed my hands with Ivory dish soap.

My baby pictures were in a narrow cardboard box in a built-in cabinet beneath the museumlike collection. Sitting on the floor, I pondered the images of him, my mother, and me. This upset him. These photos were the only evidence I had of a future that they had intended.

"There is no time for this," he told me one day. Hurt, I looked for something else to do or someplace to sit, but there really wasn't anyplace. In the corners of all the rooms, except the kitchen, were dust balls and change. I had already collected what I considered a small fortune in quarters. He had a huge dusty chair that functioned as a gothic object rather than a piece

My father in San Francisco, 1959. © Virginia Aste

of furniture. Nobody ever sat there. For a long time I thought of it as the scary chair because it looked like it had been removed from a haunted house. The chair had a high back with carved curlicue legs and a faded tapestry cover. Finally some years later the papier-mâché bird, Willard, claimed the chair as his own. Willard became the infamous bird on the cover of my father's book *Willard and His Bowling Trophies*. I liked Willard, and once he became famous he went places with us. "Even a bird needs to get out once in a while," my father said.

One memorable night when I was seventeen or so, Willard decided that he wanted to go to a dinner party at Curt Gentry's house. Curt's then ex-wife didn't like this at all, because Willard wasn't content to just sit in a chair in the corner. He wanted a drink, whiskey of course, and his own place setting. Even though I knew that Willard wasn't real and my father was interpreting his needs, some leftover child part of me thought of Willard as alive. Instead of being embarrassed, I enjoyed Willard's antics and wondered if he would ask for dessert. Poor Curt was stuck trying to ride that impossible line of finding the whole thing hysterical while trying to manage my drunk father and pacify his wife, who liked to give fancy but uneventful dinner parties.

Sleeping, because I had to sleep in my father's writing room, which frightened me at night, was a problem. He left the hall light on for me, and I liked the clean smell of the sheets and the special little bed he made for me. But I would still lie wide awake in the narrow passageway between his deck and bookshelf worrying. This worrying started after a conversation he and I had about death when I was about eight. "Turning thirty was a surprise," he said while lifting a brown mug to his lips. "I never

My mother and me, 1960. © Virginia Aste

thought I would live to be thirty." The scary thing, then and now, was that he did look amazed to be alive and standing in his kitchen talking to me. So I began a long phase of thinking about death before I went to sleep. For if someone as powerful as my father could be surprised he was alive, then how could I, a child, count on something as fundamental as my own heart continuing to beat?

Eventually, when I was eleven years old, my father got a TV. I would lug it into his writing room and set up a little nest with the feather pallet and blankets and watch Sunday-morning television, which usually meant a lot of Ma and Pa Kettle movies. This conquered the room.

He did not have any children's books. Now I'm kind of glad.

I would never have enjoyed reading the *Butch Cassidy and the Sundance Kid* script.

In 1974, because of the ongoing construction noise of the Geary Tunnel, which was being built for no apparent reason right in front of his building, my father decided to move. As soon as he left, everything changed. He drank more. Geary Street had fit him; it was a comforting place. For almost a decade, I knew exactly where my father was, and this was very important to me. Sometimes I fantasize that if he had never moved, he wouldn't have killed himself. He could have holed up there with his cheap rent and continued his life.

Except for Willard, the collection disappeared. "Packed up," he told me. I liked the newer kitchens with shiny linoleum, writing rooms that were a little less spooky, matching furniture I could sit on, and the lack of huge sheets of peeling paint hanging from the ceiling. I loved the fact that he now owned something as ordinary as a couch.

The Geary apartment is gone, torn down and replaced by condominiums, but the funky little red caboose drive-in remains on the corner, a beacon of the past. Throughout the years I would walk down to get some fries and a chili dog, first as a cautious six-year-old and then as a careless teenager, convinced that my father was invincible.

Playland

This is a constant story that I keep telling my daughter who is four years old. She gets something from it and wants to hear it again and again.

When it's time for her to go to bed, she says, "Daddy, tell me about when you were a kid and climbed inside that rock."

"OK."

She cuddles the covers about her as if they were controllable clouds and puts her thumb in her mouth and looks at me with listening blue eyes.

—R. B., "ONE AFTERNOON IN 1939,"
IN *REVENGE OF THE LAWN*

One foggy summer morning, up before anyone else, drinking coffee, I remembered Playland. Playland-at-the-Beach was an amusement park by the ocean near the zoo in San Francisco, where it was almost always overcast. Above the Fun House sat Laughing Sal, a giant animated creature in a polka-dotted dress, who lurched back and forth with a rhythmic, cackling laugh, scaring all the small children, including Cadence and me. I didn't like Sal, and I didn't like Playland very much. I was afraid of all the rides there, except for the merry-go-round. This makes me think that I was around four when my father took me there. Because when we took Elizabeth to Disneyland when she was four, she refused to go on most of the rides except for the merry-go-round. But for some reason she agreed to go on the battered submarine ride in Tomorrowland. All the little underwater tableaus were faded and worn.

After navigating past Laughing Sal, I usually picked out a horse on the merry-go-round. My father would put the little safety strap around my waist so I wouldn't fall off, and then once I was secured he stepped off to wave at me. After that we walked around, stopping to watch a few solitary people ride the roller coaster. He and I liked the sound of the roller coaster.

I asked Cadence if we could go take a look at where Playland used to be. I pictured an old abandoned amusement park on the beach waiting for me to come and take a last glance.

"If you want to go to a Safeway," she replied. "They build a Safeway and strip mall there. But if you really want to, we could go."

She was humoring me. I didn't tell her why I would like to go to the beach near Playland. I lost a bucket there once.

"When you were little," my father told me one day, "I gave you a blue bucket with a shovel and took you to the beach."

He was crafty about the past; direct questions were rarely answered. Answers that were forthcoming came with a cost. His eyes became troubled, and he might take a deep, careful breath. He warded off my questions about my parents' divorce with phrases like "Your mother and I planned you, and when you were born we were very happy." Neither he nor my mother ever spoke about their breakup. Reading pages from a notebook he kept in 1963, I found out that they had split up on Christmas Eve, which explained why I had always found the holidays difficult. My father came back that Christmas in 1963 to open presents with my mother and me, and afterwards we all went for a walk together. In the notebook the reason for their separation was not clear.

. . .

And for a long time, no matter how persistently I begged, my normally talkative father, who answered most of my questions, absolutely refused to tell me anything about his own parents. Other than a bedtime story about his childhood, which ended up in a book of short stories entitled *Revenge of the Lawn,* I didn't have any details about his mother and father. "Maybe someday," he said. But this bucket story wasn't like that. It, like other stories he was willing to tell me about my babyhood, seemed to appear from thin air.

"You were playing quietly on the beach and a sneaker wave came out of nowhere. I ran and grabbed you, but your bucket was swept out into the surf. I set you down where you would be safe and ran down to get the blue bucket because I knew that you would be upset. You really liked the bucket. I ran down to the water and began wading frantically back out into the surf trying to retrieve this bucket." (He laughed at the memory of himself in the water. I shuddered slightly at the thought of him in the water, because he was not a swimming-type dad.) "And you yelled down to me, 'Get out of the water, Daddy. The bucket is gone.'

"I realized you were right, the bucket was gone. You were a smart little girl."

Sometimes my next-door neighbors take my daughter and their son to the beach. I fret very quietly until they come back. I don't mention this to my husband, Paul. I know that I'm being ridiculous. My neighbors are strong swimmers. They would never lose her in the water.

When Elizabeth returns from a day away from home, she likes to be alone. She has lots of toys and games and endless reams of paper and crayons. But she sits in the middle of her room for remarkable lengths of time. Sometimes I lean on the doorjamb of the doorway to her room and watch her. Her long, thin fingers are entwined in her sandy, tangled hair and her back is to me.

My Father's Hair Looked like Albert Einstein's

As I go to change the calendar from June to July with its photo of Albert Einstein, I notice that my father's hair looked a bit like his. In the picture Albert's is just below his ears, curling up a bit. The year the picture was taken is 1952.

My father would have been in high school, with short hair, getting ready to discover Emily Dickinson.

After my father died, his whole life was delivered to my address, along with his heavy overcoat and a pair of rubber fishing boots. The coat went to the basement, the boots to the garage. One day, when I finally had the courage to look at the coat, I noticed strands of his wispy blond hair on the collar. The hair looked very alive, as though he had been wearing the coat only a moment ago, gotten hot, and decided to take it off.

After a big rainstorm, his rubber fishing boots migrated into the house. They come in handy to slip on in the winter when I go out to catch the bunny. We let our rabbit run around the backyard during the day and put him in a cage at night. Since my husband had a pair that looked similar, for a while I thought the boots were his. They're not.

When I was a little girl I used to wear my father's shoes around his apartment, convinced that someday my feet would be as big as his. Since he wore size thirteen, this was impossible, but he didn't inform me of this fact. He let me believe my feet could grow as large as his.

The Nature of Suicide

I've been honest with my daughter about her grandfather's death. Because he died before she was born, I wasn't sure how to tell her about his suicide. I didn't want her to hear about it from someone else at school. As soon as I thought she was old enough, at six years old, I told her.

"You know Grandpa is dead."

"Yes."

"He committed suicide."

"What's suicide?"

"It's when you take your life."

She nodded, and I thought I had gotten over the worst of it.

"How?"

"Well, he had some problems."

"No," she said, interrupting me. "How? A knife? A rope?"

"Oh," I said, racking my brains for a moment or two trying to figure out how to make a gun not sound so horrible. I gave up.

"A gun."

"How did he do it?" she said, putting her fingers in a cocked position like a gun, holding them up and waving them through the air. This I definitely wasn't ready for.

"His head," I said quickly before she figured that out.

"Where on his head?"

"We don't know for sure," I said.

She relaxed her fingers.

The nature of suicide is that it is shameful. Families usually lie about it. A lot of suicides are not recorded as such. I didn't realize how much I blamed myself until the father of a family I only knew vaguely killed himself, leaving a sixteen-year-old boy behind.

"I wonder what they did wrong," I found myself thinking.

This shocked me, and I cried.

In the first grade at my daughter's school, they have "Person of the Week." Each child gets a poster board to display pictures of their family on, and the child talks about the pictures.

"How did it go?" I asked her.

"Fine," she said.

I winced as a thought went through my head. Not wanting to be obvious, I began inching toward the question.

"What did you say about Grandma Ginny?"

"She lives in Hawaii and sends me things."

"What did you say about Dad?"

"He edits things and directs commercials."

"What did you say about Grandpa?"

"That he shot himself in the head with a gun."

"What did your teacher say?"

"'Oh.'"

While I was writing this Elizabeth woke up and came in with her favorite blanket wrapped around her shoulders.

"'The Nature of,'" she read on my page, and halted. I was hoping that her third-grade reading vocabulary wouldn't include this word. It did. "'Suicide,'" she finished. I sat, not sure of what to say.

"That title has a nice ring to it."

I forced myself not to evade the topic. "What do you think suicide means?" We hadn't talked about this in a long time.

"It's what Grandpa did to himself."

"Why do you think he did that?"

"Because he had problems from his life. And the alcohol pushed him over the edge." She repeated the word for emphasis: "Pushed." She smiled and looked closely at me, gave me a little hug and a pat on the shoulder.

"Sort of like my teeth," she added.

"How?" I asked, somewhat alarmed.

"There are too many and they're getting pushed around." She opened her mouth to show me what I and the orthodontist knew.

Fame

On my ninth birthday, my father bought me a bike. He and some friends drove up to the dilapidated farm where I was living with my mother, my half-sisters, Ellen and Mara, and soon-to-be-born half-brother, Jess. He took me to the Schwinn dealership, and I picked out a bike. I don't remember any of the people that came with him. He was extraordinarily pleased to buy the bike, and I, in turn, loved the gift. It had a sparkly purple seat and came with built-in headlights, which, of course, stopped working right away, but the bike lasted forever. He insisted I try it out. At first I was embarrassed to be driving around a parking lot in front of him and his friends. But the moment I felt the speed I created, they were forgotten.

He was very famous by then. I didn't realize this. I just wished that he could stay longer, but of course he couldn't. The smiling, gracious people were taking him somewhere else. I consoled myself knowing he was now only a bus ride away.

The rest of the birthday was a good one, except now I can feel the ache in my arms as I waved after the car that took him away one more time.

The thirty-five acres of fields surrounding the farm were woven with wildflowers, which I thought were a personal gift to me from a cosmic source that had nothing to do with the loneliness that threatened to overtake me, but existed solely to give remarkable gifts like sunny, warm days. I walked tentatively that day through the thick, green grass. The day ended with a white sheet cake with tiny plastic ballerinas holding lit candles. My mother gave me a diary. I wrote a few things before losing it. Because then, and sometimes now, it took, and takes, all my energy to hold on to my father and the small hope that the spring gave me. Small hope goes a long way in my body.

This year, 1995, on my birthday, my mother sent me pale roses, the color of dawn, surrounded by small white daisies and ferns. Daisies were my father's favorite flower. I held the vase easily in one hand, even though it was a large one. Hope need not weigh much.

Beyond Words

Sometimes the love I have for my father overtakes my whole being, and I want to leap into the air and grab onto whatever color is there to express how my heart feels. At times like those I envision myself as a sort of sky acrobat, swinging from handhold to handhold in the blue atmosphere. This love is not weak and doesn't fail and remains forever mine.

Cannibal Carpenters

That's what my father called biographers, yet he loved to read biographies of his favorite writers. He had a huge two-volume one about William Faulkner. He gave me a memoir written by Faulkner's mistress. I found a memoir written by Hemingway's wife among his books. I opened it up and had to put it away because there was a picture of a sad, alcoholic Hemingway sitting in a bathtub.

Together one afternoon around 1977 when I was seventeen we looked through a book, *Hollywood Babylon.* I asked him about the suicide of a young actress in the book, to which he replied:

"Here she thought that she was going to be found lying in a bed of beautiful flowers and instead she was found with her head in the toilet. It's a shame. After all that careful planning that's where she died."

My father set timers in his house before he killed himself. For a long time the radio played, the lights went on and off dutifully as each night passed, and his answering machine filled up until it could hold no more messages. Maybe he did this so it would be such a horror show that romantically inclined young poets wouldn't be tempted to follow in his path. Maybe he was about to go on a trip and decided to kill himself instead. Maybe it was all a big fat fucking mistake. Maybe. Maybe. The cannibals are making up lots of reasons, taking his bones and piling them one way and then another. They call me sometimes. They are always very nice to me before they ask me questions. "I've got an arm here, Ianthe, do you know where the leg is?" They seem to think that my heart is made of stone.

Tonight, late, as I was going through some of his unpublished poetry I found myself looking for a sign, a note, something to tell me why. For a few seconds my heart beat fast, and I actually thought I might find a reason. I didn't. They were just poems, not reasons.

> *We listened to the voyages of angels*
> *across frozen fields of flowers. We*
> *listened as their boats sailed toward*
> *distant, dreaming*
> *towers. We listened . . .*
>
> —R. B., FRAGMENT OF
> AN UNPUBLISHED POEM

The Promised Land

Occasionally, my father visits me in my dreams. While I'm awake he is dead, but as soon as I fall asleep he arrives. Being logical, I ask him how this is possible. "I saw you dead," which is a lie, because I didn't exactly see all of him dead, just the blood. He lies right back, "The CIA, they can do that sort of thing."

"Fake death?"

"Yep."

And I believe this until I wake up, and he is dead again.

About a year ago things changed. He came to visit in a dream, answered questions about writing, gave me a little advice, and made me laugh. For however few seconds it takes a dream to run, all was well.

Now, I see that this was just a glimpse of the Promised Land, and I see that I'm still in the desert listening for rattlesnakes and trying not to step on scorpions, wondering how long I can avoid the pain.

Copying

As a tired thirteen-year-old, I sat on the floor of a drugstore in North Beach, leaning up against a copy machine. Back then it took a while to photocopy an entire manuscript. I knew better than to talk to my father, because the exactness of the process made him irritable. There was no placing the pile of white paper in a slot and pressing a button. One sheet at a time. Insert the coin. No copy cards. Then wait for the slowly moving light to flash across the document.

The whole afternoon seemed to pass waiting for my father to finish doing this. I fidgeted with my new purse. Nothing in it but a comb and a buck. In my state of relief that he was finally dong copying, I jumped up and forgot the purse. I didn't notice this until we got back to his place.

"Was there anything important in it? We could go back, but it's probably gone now."

I shook my head. I liked the purse, but I knew he was right.

An hour bus ride seemed like a long time to spend retrieving something that was most likely gone. I let the purse go. I had learned long ago that there was no going back with my father. We moved in one direction.

The Acute Phase

I lived through four of my father's acute phases. He only made it through three. An acute phase is a period of time during which someone suicidal is in danger of hurting himself.

When I was about eight, he began talking about death. At fourteen he told me the only reason he didn't kill himself was that he didn't want me to find his body. Each time he managed to pull himself together and go on once more while I could only stand by helpless.

I got better and better at separating the two sides of my father. There was the father that I could call on in times of trouble, the father who knew everything and loved me. When I became a teenager, the other father began to color the night black with his pain. At the age of twenty I was reduced to begging him over the phone in the middle of the night not to kill himself. "Please, Daddy, please Daddy," I cried. He hung up the phone, leaving me trembling and alone in the kitchen. For a long time my eyes clung to the tiny light coming from the glowing dial on the electric stove.

Tragedy with Two Coats

Two coats sit out on the railing of the back porch. Both were my father's. One is a heavy gray-and-black overcoat and the other is a navy–royal blue suede with silver snaps at the wrists. The snaps stand out because my father rarely snapped them. His pale wrists always poked out under the edges of the unsnapped sleeves. I held his hand many times, while he wore that coat, my face rubbing on the sleeve with the snaps, smelling the suede and enjoying its soft texture against my cheek. It's hard for me to believe that I was ever that small.

When my father came down to California from the rainy Pacific Northwest, he brought with him the layered look, what we now call "grunge." The weather changes so often that you dress in a T-shirt and then a long-sleeved shirt and then a sort of sweater and then a coat.

His skin was extremely white, so any kind of tanning was out of the question. I never saw him sunburned because he was so careful. He couldn't swim, or so he said. I watched him one extraordinary afternoon floundering around in a pond, standing up every so often in the cold shallow water, to announce he was, indeed, swimming. I felt a tad bit betrayed because he always swore he couldn't swim a stroke and here he was sort of swimming.

He told me when we went to Key West, he swam at night. All the men we were with were very tan and wore Top-Siders without any socks. My father always wore socks.

He rigged up an outfit, including a hat to protect his face, and managed not to expose any of his white skin to the sun. This enabled him to go out onto the Keys and fish tarpon. I, having my mother's skin, was able to sit by the pool in a pretty suit that Tom McGuane's wife, Becky, gave me. I was so shy that I never was able to tell her how beautiful I thought the bathing suit was.

My only escape from the bathing beauties was occasionally slipping down to the beach and swimming in the warm salt water.

"Watch out for barracuda," my father told me.

I opened my eyes underwater in the hope of seeing one, but I never got lucky. I wanted to go tarpon fishing but was told that fourteen-year-old girls weren't allowed. This unfairness and the tropics affected my skin, and I broke out in a heat rash.

My father, trying to relieve my misery, took me on a long walk to an air-conditioned movie theater. The movie was Spanish and had no subtitles. We stayed in the cool, soothing building until the last credits rolled and then wandered back to the house in the almost-dark, quiet streets of Key West. By the time we arrived, the house was lit up and filled with people, Tom and his wife, Becky, and a French documentary film crew brought over to America by Guy de la Valdène. We all ate huge plates of shrimp. I fell asleep to the sound of talking and lots of laughter.

"I'm taking the stuff we cleared out of the basement," my husband called out to me in his I'm-cleaning-up tone of voice.

"Don't take the coats," I yelled. "I'm not ready for you to take the coats."

Now, they sit in the baking summer sun. Paul wore his dead grandfather's heavy wool overcoat when we lived in New York. I would like to think that someone could get some use out of my father's coats, but a part of me thinks they are tainted. For some odd reason, I think that suicide is contagious, and if I were to give them to a grandchild the child might be infected. I know rationally that I can't catch death, but there is still a part of me that feels that somehow my father's blood covers everything. I try to remember that coats are just coats. It's not their fault that my father, in a moment of despair, succeeded in killing himself.

I think I am going to get the coats cleaned. They can hang for another six years until my husband calls out to me from the basement. I will shout out to him, "No, leave the coats." He will set them on the porch railing, and perhaps that day I will know what do with them.

The IBM

His IBM Selectric sat on a big dark oak table at Geary Street, covered with a plastic fitted cover. Sharpened pencils lay on one of their hexagonal sides, neatly lined up alongside little piles of correcting tape and stacks of what he was writing. He never had to tell me not to touch that paper; those white sheets were more important than anything I could think of and meant a great deal to my father.

"Can I type?" I asked when I was six.

"Not now" was the usual answer, but this time he carefully sat me down at the desk and put two pieces of paper in the typewriter, turning his head to stare at me with an instructive look in his eye. "You can wreck the platen if you don't put two pieces in." Impatient. "No. No. One key at a time. Don't bang. Careful. There."

I was left alone. The room grew silent except for the hum of the typewriter. For a long time it loomed over me and even scared me a little. My feet didn't touch the floor, so I sort of floated until I reached forward to press a key, always shocked at the sound of the key hitting the paper. I typed my name and a few words and then sat still, not quite knowing what to do next with the blank piece of typing paper.

I knew that this typewriter was the door to a different world that my father inhabited from time to time. I'd look around at the high ceiling, bookshelves overflowing, torn blue bedspread covering the tall dirty window shutting out the outside, sitting under the large overhead light, trying to find a clue to enter this mysterious place my father went. What I found strange was that he acted like this was a perfectly ordinary room, while I knew otherwise. I'd watched him carefully for a long time, sure he would give away the secret the room held, but he never did. Occasionally, I would push open the door to his little closet, which held his few clothes, to see if it went somewhere else. There was just an ordinary wall.

So this large tan humming machine was the gateway. I was convinced if I could figure out the secret of the machine I could go there. Again and again throughout the years, I sat at the typewriter looking at the keys for a clue.

A small black binder given to me by my tutor, Helen Seacat, solved the mystery. She was a kind woman hired by my father when I was eleven years old to teach me to spell. It was a task I failed, although I did begin to write in the binder I was supposed to copy my spelling words in. With the aid of a real fountain pen that was supposed to help me have better handwriting, I first heard my voice on the page. Shocked and delighted, I continued to write, happy to be alive.

I now understood the secret. It wasn't the machine; the world existed in my father. Most people were all on the outside, while he existed mostly in his imagination. Instead of going to an office and working, he went for long walks inside himself using his body as a map. His books became comforting to me. Even if, at eleven, I didn't understand all the stories in them, someday I would.

I could never make the IBM look the same when I tried to put it away. My six-year-old fingers were unable to place the cover on the typewriter without having it look awkward.

Going to find my father, I said, "I'm done."

"Did you turn it off and put the cover on?"

"Yes."

"Good. Let me see. Very nice. Good work."

He bought me my own typewriter when I was nine years old. It was a black Royal portable.

The typewriter now holds a place of honor beside my computer. My daughter has her eye on it. The Royal is the perfect size for a nine-year-old. Occasionally, I let her type on it, and the carrying case is just the right size to keep trolls in. She will be nine in September, and I will pass it on to her. I wonder if she will feel the same combination of wonder and frustration that was the catalyst for me to keep searching for the place my father knew so well.

Now his tan IBM Selectric sits under its cover in the attic, nowhere near a plug because I know that the temptation might be too great for him.

The Whole Man

Memories drift to the ground like snow, and I can see my father with me as a teenager. He stands slightly crooked because of the scoliosis in his back, and his fingers, expressive yet contained, nails bitten down to the quick, rest on his hip, until he moves. And then he is walking, looking straight ahead, and we are going to the movies in San Francisco on a Saturday afternoon. The sky is overcast and will still be when we get out. He picks out seats in the near-empty theater, and I go and get some popcorn. We are there early. My father has a thing about time and he likes to get places ahead of time. So we sit looking at the darkened screen for a good fifteen minutes. Neither of us wears a watch, so we are suspended within a part of the day that can't be accounted for. The movie starts and both of us are changed by it; *Chinatown*. We leave even more quiet than when we came in. The gray of the sidewalks and the sky seems sad.

The two of us spent a great deal of time in movie theaters together in my childhood. He thought that this was a suitable activity for a father and daughter, except that we never saw anything remotely resembling a children's movie. This was not due to my lack of trying. I would take the pink section, the *Chronicle's* entertainment guide, and sit on the floor and point out movies I wanted to see. *Swiss Family Robinson* was rejected in favor of *Slaughterhouse-Five,* or *Amarcord,* and for a brief horrifying period of time we went to nothing but Japanese samurai pictures. And I learned to like them; I especially liked the Blind Swordsman films. Sometimes we went mainstream. We became hysterical with laughter while watching *Sleeper.* During *Young Frankenstein,* my father was laughing so hard that he dipped his hand in what he thought was his popcorn but turned out to be his large soft drink. His soda spilled and his wild, whooping laughter filled the theater. I laughed so hard while watching *City Lights* that my stomach hurt. We walked out on *Manhattan.* He tapped me on the shoulder, and we left the theater and finished our popcorn on the way home. I didn't know anyone else who walked out of movies other than my father.

Only once did he ask me if he had gone too far, and that was during *The Rocky Horror Picture Show.* The movie had just come out. He turned to me during the Transylvanian transvestite number and said, "Are you old enough to see this movie?" I was fifteen and nodded my head.

When I was twenty and we were at his ranch in Montana, he spent an hour or so one cool fall morning explaining to me how to go about writing a screenplay. He was about to go on a book tour for *The Tokyo–Montana Express.* I think screenwriting was a skill that he thought was a good idea for me to know how to do, sort of like typing. His friends were doing well in this regard. What my father wanted was what some close friends had, their literary novels sold to producers and made into movies. Movie money, for a writer, made for a certain sense of security. I think part of what he needed was safety, but turning to Hollywood for this was not a great idea. His books were optioned by some wonderful people but nothing ever came of anything. We had both seen and loved *Being There,* directed by Hal Ashby. And so when Ashby purchased the rights to *The Hawkline Monster* it was very exciting. But not too much later, my father told me sadly that the word out of Hollywood was that Ashby was ill and unable to work.

He also told me that he had been invited to Jack Nicholson's house. This was unusual for him because he rarely told me about famous people that he had met. But he knew that I really liked the movie *Chinatown.*

"What was it like?"

"Well, Harry Dean Stanton took me there, and I got drunk and shot baskets."

"And?"

"I don't think Jack liked me very much."

"Why?"

"I decided to make a point in my conversation that required more than just words. So I took a bunch of lilies from a vase and tossed them in the air."

I could understand Jack Nicholson was probably irritated at my father for getting drunk in his beautiful Hollywood home. He had wanted to meet the electrically brilliant Richard Brautigan and instead here was a drunken writer messing up his house. But I can see the beautiful thick green stocks of lilies flying up towards the ceiling, spraying little droplets of water everywhere, and then Harry Dean scrambling to pick up the flowers on the perfect floor while my father moved on to some new disaster. At the time the story made me sorry, because I

Happy Acres

Happy Acres was the name of the old folks' home I was going to send my father to when he got old and misbehaved.

"No, no, don't send me to Happy Acres," he would say in his quavery old-man imitation.

"Daddy, it's for your own good."

"I'll be good, I promise."

"You'll have lots of new friends."

"Noooooooooo," he would screech, and hobble out of the room.

Close to the Ceiling

Elizabeth walked into the living room wearing a dress Paul bought me fourteen years ago. She's a tall girl, so it almost fit her.

"Look what I found," she said.

"Your dad gave me that for Christmas before you were born."

"You fit into this dress?" she said.

"Yes."

The dress hung on her frame, and the buttons on the back were fastened out of order.

"Let me fix the buttons," I said.

She went away and came back with a pair of long johns.

"Look, more neat stuff," she said.

I jumped up from the couch, my stomach in a knot.

"Where are you finding this stuff?"

"In the drawers in the hallway," she said, looking at me with her clear blue eyes.

I tried to keep my voice casual. "You know, I think you have found enough stuff for one night."

"I can't reach the top drawers."

"Mm-hmm," I said, keeping my face neutral.

"I'm finding all this neat stuff."

"Well, it's time to go to bed." I stood there and wondered if she would drop the idea of exploring the drawers' contents.

Elizabeth shifted focus and went off to brush her teeth.

I realized I was going to have to move my father soon.

The top drawer near the ceiling was no longer safe.

I wonder if I'll ever be able to bury him or if I will just keep finding new hiding places around the house for him. Can you keep someone dead for a long time? It's not like I keep him on the mantel or the coffee table. I never talk to him. He just has a warm, dry place to be where I know he is comfortable, listening to the sounds of his granddaughter playing, the dishwasher running, and basketball games on the TV. I like having him around. My husband doesn't mind. The drawer was his idea. "I'm *not* vacuuming up your father if there is an earthquake."

There is only one problem with keeping my father: my daughter. Is she going to find it extremely odd when she finds out? And when do I tell her? How old does one need to be in order to be told that the ashes of one's grandfather reside in a drawer close to the ceiling?

Bolinas

Cadence has believed that the Bolinas house was haunted since the first time she saw it. We were twelve years old. She took one look at the three-story Arts and Crafts–style house, which was set back in a steep hillside, and quickly came to her decision. Cadence had driven down with my mother to pick me up after I had spent a long weekend with my dad. She refused to go into the house. Cadence was the bravest person I knew and, like me, had lived in lots of old houses. I wanted her to come in so I could show her around, but she wouldn't budge. None of the grown-ups noticed that she just hung out by the car waiting. This had a huge impact on me. Not only because it echoed my own feelings about the house but also because Cadence had never before pronounced a house haunted.

Not long after, I found out that there was a real ghost. A Chinese woman who had worked as a servant for the original owners of the house had killed herself, and some people said her spirit frequented the house. The house's appearance didn't help matters. It was covered with dark shingles and overgrown with vines. Enormous trees towered over the property. Although my father had a tree service in to prune any dead branches, he refused to trim the trees or cut back any of the foliage. At night it was absolutely pitch dark and difficult to find the front door or back door. Not long after this my father broke his leg walking in broad daylight from the back door to the front of the property. I asked him how he did this, expecting a long dramatic story. Instead he let out a sigh and said, "I just tripped on a root."

He hated having a broken leg. Navigating everywhere on crutches was difficult for him. He did a lot of hopping around the Geary apartment, the sight of which made me giggle. My mother sent him vitamins and health food drinks, which, to my surprise, he consumed. He wanted to heal as soon as possible. Hopping got old very fast, he told me.

In the Bolinas house there were three floors. The top floor had two dark servant bedrooms, a bath, and two nice bedrooms separated by a landing. The second floor had an enormous kitchen with giant pantry and a dark, cramped servants' stairway leading up to the third floor. On the same floor there was also a big living room with a walk-in fireplace, another staircase, and a small bedroom and bath right next to French doors which led out onto a wonderful deck. The bottom floor had a musty-smelling master bedroom, the only full bath in the house, and an ancient heater. My father slept down there once in a while, but nobody else went down there much except to bathe.

The first extended periods of time I spent with my dad began in Bolinas. I was eleven years old. He let me choose a bedroom and surprised me with Mickey Mouse sheets and a happy-face nightlight.

Me on the deck at the Bolinas house, 1971. © Ianthe Brautigan Swensen

On a Friday night over Easter vacation, he wanted to watch the Lakers game and I wanted to watch *The Brady Bunch.* So he made a bet with me. The deal was that whoever won would get to watch the program of their choice. We did a lot of wagering together. I got most of my allowance raises from winning bets. We turned anything into a contest: which elevator door would open first was a favorite pastime. Betting with my father often involved elaborate preparation. It was about six in the evening and we were on the hillside at dusk collecting pinecones for the TV bet. As the night grew darker, while we searched for the perfect-sized pinecone, he teased me, sure he was going to win. He carefully set up a metal wastepaper basket as a makeshift basketball hoop and then measured out the distance we had to shoot from. Whoever could make three baskets in a row with pinecones got control of the television. He let me win and I was allowed to watch my program, only cutting to the game during commercials.

Nighttime in the house was a problem. I was convinced the ghost was going to come and visit me. For a while, the happy-face nightlight protected me up there on the third floor. But the house was made of redwood and when it contracted at night it sounded like legions of Odysseus' dead were wandering around the upper floors.

I finally became so terrified that I asked my father if I could change bedrooms. He moved me to the little one on the second floor, which was nearer to him. This was better, except that now I was sure that the ghosts were coming down the stairs to get me. I thought it was the mirror hanging on the lower-landing wall that stopped ghosts. To make things worse, the electricity would go off for an hour or so at a time and with it my happy-face nightlight.

Daylight changed everything for me. I liked the Bolinas house in the daytime. I put on records and squeezed fresh orange juice for my dad or watched one of his girlfriends make pancakes. I learned to bake chocolate cakes and went exploring. On the third floor I could travel from one of the bedrooms into another by slipping into the closet, which had a secret passageway. My father avoided *all* the bedrooms and for a long time slept in the huge living room next to the walk-in fireplace.

I played an out-of-tune piano and spent hours with dead tennis balls and old rackets, beating the balls against the backboard at the local tennis court. Down by the beach I was intrigued and disappointed by the band who lived in a house there, the Jefferson Airplane, I think. I wanted to see them so badly, but they were never home. Each time I came to Bolinas, I hoped that this time the band would be home and someone famous would come

My father standing by the window, eating a plum, Bolinas, 1971.
© Ianthe Brautigan Swensen

to that gate and use the speakerphone, but no one ever did. It never occurred to me that my father's house was filled with its own kind of famous people. They were mostly poets, like Robert Creeley, who on occasion loved to drink and stay up all night long. I liked it when they held marathons of this sort, because it meant that the evenings were filled with a kind of foot-stomping, boisterous noise that chased all my kid fears away.

The cupboards in the house were filled with lots of 1930s and 1940s *Reader's Digest*s and vintage movie magazines. It seemed odd to me that a family would leave so much interesting stuff there. There were even letters in an upstairs dresser written during World War II to a Polly. I was charmed by the name Polly, which seemed both exotic and steadfast. The third floor wasn't scary in the daytime. There was a huge beehive that buzzed by one of the windows and lots of sunshine. I liked sitting up there by myself, enjoying the quiet and the musty smell of the magazines as I turned the pages. My father found a book in one of the bookshelves with my name in it. *Wedded and Parted* by Charlotte Braeme, written in about 1901. I had only seen my name once in a book: a dedication to me in my father's book *A Confederate General from Big Sur.* I had learned to take my name for granted. My father told me that Ianthe was a violet that grew on a mythological mountain and that the poet Shelley had named one of his daughters Ianthe. My parents, realizing that I might not be as delighted with such an unusual name, took the precaution of giving me Elizabeth as a middle name. And they always made it clear that I was free to change my name if I chose.

I had never met anyone with my name, so to discover a character in a book named after me was a bit startling. I knew that the betting odds of this occurring were not great. Lady Ianthe is the heroine in *Wedded and Parted.* Her father, the earl, makes bad investments and they lose all their money. Her father becomes terribly despondent. Lady Ianthe saves the ailing earl by marrying for money, not love.

"I love only my father," she tells her future husband.

When I was fourteen my father bought the ranch in Montana, and we stopped going to Bolinas together. I was twenty-four when he shot himself with a .44 Magnum on the second floor of the Bolinas house near the walk-in fireplace. He was standing up, facing the ocean. There is a corner of my mind that won't let go of the vision. I know that the light at night in that corner of the living room is dim and has a warmish glow to it. I know the cool feel of the brown leather couches that he stood near. I know the smell of that house, a mixture of redwood, ocean breeze, and musty, dry oldness. I am here, and he is there.

The night my father's death hit the news in 1984, Cadence envisioned driving to Bolinas and splashing the house with gas and setting it on fire. She blamed the house. A few days later, I went to Bolinas with my husband, my mother, and my husband's parents. They went into the house to collect my father's papers, while I sat in the car and cried.

Even though my parents had been divorced for a long time, my mother needed to go into the house and say good-bye. "It's not so bad," she tried to reassure me. Like Cadence many years before, I couldn't bring myself to enter the house. I sat in the safety of the car and stared for a long time at the window that he glanced out of before he died. Then I saw butterflies, hundreds and hundreds of orange monarch butterflies hovering. They streamed out of the stone chimney and covered that side of the house.

When I was a child my father loved to point out monarch butterflies to me.

"Look," he would whisper in the same reverent tone most men use when they spot a beautiful sports car, "a butterfly." I held my breath until the creature had drifted out of sight. After his death the butterflies had formed a cloud so large that I stopped crying. And when we all drove away leaving the empty house, they stayed.

Today, the house has been remodeled, the dark redwood walls painted. The tall dead trees have been removed and lots of flowers planted. A baby has been born there. You can see the ocean from the deck. One day I even managed to walk into the house and stay for about a minute. I forced myself to look at the corner of the living room where my father killed himself and found, to my relief, that he wasn't there.

The Power of Mother

A fter the phone call, after finding the body, after the police, came the moving. My father-in-law packed up everything in the house and moved it to mine. Some things stayed outside. He hung my father's nylon luggage set under the trees to air out. A lot of things went to the garage, but the boxes and boxes of papers were neatly stacked in the spare bedroom. He even brought the groceries from the cupboard. And the flies.

I thought I was safe because I stayed outside the house where he lay dead. My husband found a tape with piano music that my father had been playing before he died. I remembered the music. It had been written just for him back in a time when people cared to do things like that for him.

Finally, back at home in the dark, I decided to go to bed. Light, Dark, Day, Night, Life, Death. My husband had left for a few hours. I'm okay, I told him. So it was my mother who carefully walked me along the brick walkway from the big house, where my in-laws lived, though the trees, to the cottage that my husband and I lived in. Since her arrival from Hawaii, she rarely left my side. When I opened the front door, I could see a faint light shining from the bathroom. I walked past shadowy living-room furniture towards the bathroom. I knew that I was going to brush my teeth and then walk back with my mother to the big house because I couldn't be alone.

Surrounded by the apple-green walls and tile that had been so popular thirty years ago, I carefully put some toothpaste on my toothbrush. As I began to brush my teeth, I avoided looking at the mirror and glanced up instead. At first, they looked like a new wallpaper border, but I knew this didn't make sense. I looked closer and realized they were flies, hundreds and hundreds of flies. They had awakened and crawled out of the boxes of papers we had brought from the Bolinas house. They gathered in the bathroom, attracted by the light.

Still holding fast to my toothbrush, I ran past my mother and flew out the open door. My mother sprinted after me. She caught my arm.

I threw the toothbrush out into the darkness and began spitting. She twisted my arm behind my back so that I couldn't move and held me to her chest.

"I'm going to die. I'm going to die," I cried, almost unable to breathe, trying to spit out my life along with the contamination. Her strong fingers dug into my arm as I struggled against her.

"You can't catch death," she whispered in my ear. "You can't catch death."

Help

My mother-in-law drove me to San Jose to see a renowned expert on suicide. She was fitting me in between her other appointments. She had a plane to catch. I still have her card. I have fingered it so often throughout the last ten years that it's worn and the corners are bent and soft like leather. I don't remember my mother-in-law asking me if that was what I wanted to do. I just was in the car and then we were there. The building was modern and low with lots of bustling inside. Once I got to the expert's office the busyness got more intense. The phone punctuated everything. File folders full of papers danced on her desk as the shut door resounded with knocks.

She looked at me. And when she wasn't answering the phone or talking to the people that came to the door, she asked me questions. I told her my story.

"I think that you are not grieving a father."

It was my turn to stare at her.

"I think you are a mother grieving a lost son."

This made me cry because it was true.

"Where is he?"

I started to explain that he was still in the urn and that I hadn't had time to . . .

She interrupted me.

"You've got him now, don't you?"

I looked at her puzzled for a moment, and then I realized what she meant.

The phones ceased, the papers were stilled, and nobody knocked on the door.

"He's finally safe," she said.

I nodded my head as the tears rolled down my chin.

She handed me her card. "Call me if you need me."

I watched as everything fell into motion once again. We stood, and she reached out and shook my hand. I said good-bye.

Her phone started ringing again, and I had to squeeze by someone coming into the room. But I could feel her eyes still on me as I walked out the door.

Talking

I remember the cold rainy winter that followed my father's death watching the pool sweep pushing the dead leaves around on the surface of the water. Each day after he died contained a kind of grayness that weighed down my soul. My mother-in-law gave us tickets to the opera.

"You need to get out."

She took me up to her closet and dressed me in a fancy taffeta dress with satin shoes.

There were no epiphanies. I don't even recall the name of the opera, not a note of music or a word that was sung stayed in my head.

"Stop wiggling," my husband whispered. "Your dress is making noise and if you don't stop the people on the left are going to kill you."

I turned to look and they were glaring at me. I wiggled just once more and was surprised to hear how loud my dress really was.

I spent the rest of the evening holding still, trying not to move.

When I was twelve my father took me to see Nureyev in
Swan Lake at the same San Francisco Opera House. He was very
excited.

"We have great seats. We are going to see one of the world's
greatest dancers."

The lights dimmed. The opening party scene began. The
dancers were toasting each other with empty goblets onstage.

"When do they start talking?" my father murmured after
about ten minutes.

"They don't."

"Not ever?"

"No."

"No talking?"

"They just dance."

A long silence.

"I'm going to go get a drink. I'll meet you at the downstairs
bar after it's over."

I sat alone in the dark with the dancers.

Afterwards he was there waiting, easy to find, faded blue
jeans, long hair, awkward and yet as graceful as Nureyev.

"There has to be talking. That's what people do, they talk,"
he said as we walked against the cold wind that always blows
down Van Ness.

Blood and Hope

I heard a writer talk about writing. She said that writers bleed metaphorically on the page.

I have a lot of paper with blood on it, because when my father killed himself he bled on some of the pages he'd been working on. In the beginning, I washed my hands a lot when handling his papers, as if that would somehow help. But even the scent of soap can't cover up a suicide.

As I read the words alongside the dried bits of tissue and see the marks of maggots, which fed on my father, I sit and look up at the light on the ceiling and wonder what keeps me here.

On my first wedding anniversary, before my father died, I stabbed myself in the thigh a couple of times with a Gerber steak knife, a wedding gift. It is an understatement to say that this did not make my new husband happy. He bandaged me up and refused to let me cancel a walking tour of the ship *Intrepid* the next day. I limped along for hours with my husband and his brother.

My father refused to come to my wedding. He thought I was too young to get married. I paid a terrible price for defying him.

I knew he was dying. There was no blood then, only angry drunken phone calls in the middle of the night. I could see the end of his life again, and I was filled with so much pain and helplessness that I tried to mask it with the point of a knife, hoping that one pain would cancel out the other.

My in-laws planned a perfect wedding. My father raged. I convinced myself, for a moment, that I was escaping his death.

Lost Child

Sometimes I would go to a grocery store to study English. I would walk up and down the aisles reading the labels off cans. There were pictures on the cans which helped a lot. I would look at the picture of some peas on a can and read the word peas *and put it together. I would hang around the canned fruit section and learn peaches, cherries, plums, pears, oranges and pineapple. I learned my fruits very quickly after I had made the big decision that I wanted out of the first grade.*

—R. B., "Farewell to the First Grade
and Hello to the *National Enquirer*,"
in *The Tokyo–Montana Express*

I volunteer at my daughter's school helping small, shy children learn to read. Some of the second-graders are simply not quite ready and others just haven't had anyone to help them with this endeavor. Together we hope. In the middle of the semester most who couldn't read now can. In the beginning they were not so sure that this was going to work, but they were willing to share my and the teacher's faith. Last week a little girl read to me a book she took delight in. As she read and we chuckled together at the story, she looked up at me to confirm her ability. I nodded my head, and confirmed that yes indeed, she was reading.

My child can read. My child has parents capable of taking care of her. My child gets enough to eat and has clean clothes to wear.

My father had none of these things. He was considered just another dirty-white-trash child. While he didn't know how to help me with my schoolwork, he did go out of his way to make sure that I wore clothes to school that no one would laugh at.

The Sound of Death

I started being afraid of guns when my father bought a .357 Magnum. He liked to fire it with his friends in the early evening off the back porch of the ranch, aiming towards the mountains. I found the best thing to do was to shut all the doors to the outside and crouch on the floor in the middle of the house with my hands covering my ears so that the sound would not be so loud. The gun had a good-sized kick, so they didn't shoot it for long. Everyone got a turn and then the pistol was carefully put away. My father made a big deal about handling the gun. You always checked to see if it was loaded before you handed it over to the next person and then they checked. I hated guns. Once I felt I could trust the silence, I would open my eyes and take my fingers out of my ears and slowly stand up.

For a while after my father's death, I worked the triage line for a large HMO, and one Saturday I had a suicide call. I kept a young woman on the phone for thirty minutes until the police arrived.

"No," she corrected me, "I didn't say I attempted to hurt myself. I tried to kill myself."

"When?" I said.

"Two weeks ago. But today I'm thinking about doing the same thing."

"Why?" I asked her.

When the police knocked on her door, she asked me what to do.

"Go answer the door," I said, feeling really bad at deceiving her. But when she went on to say that would be rather difficult because she had nailed the front door shut, I knew I was doing the right thing.

"Tell whoever it is to meet you at the back door."

"That's a good idea."

An officer got on the phone with me and asked me why he had been called. I told him that the woman had told me she wanted to hurt herself.

I heard him fumble with the receiver. "No, we're not here to arrest you. Do you want to go to the hospital and talk to someone?" he said to her.

"She's going with us," he said to me and then hung up. I stayed on the line for a moment listening to the silence.

The first summer I spent at the ranch in Montana, I arrived to find a framed shot-out clock in the kitchen. My father and a friend had sat up drinking all night long and shot out all the hours. In the place of twelve o'clock was a bullet hole. One o'clock was a bullet hole, and so on. It was expensive to fix the structural damage, because the bullets ripped all the way through the back of the house. But the surface bullet holes were

Bullet holes in the ranch house kitchen. © Ianthe Brautigan Swensen

never filled. Instead, they were framed. Before I came that first summer, part of the ceiling in the kitchen had been replaced above the sink because my father had gone at it with an ax. The contractor had just finished the remodeling when my father did this. Everything was repaired by the time I arrived, all except for the clock, which had a brass plaque. It read:

SHOOT-OUT AT OK KITCHEN. *R.B. and P.D.*

My father had a friend of his teach me how to shoot a small .22-caliber rifle. My father didn't come with us. He was rather grim about the whole thing. The gun was beautiful and surprisingly light. But it scared me, I didn't want to learn how to shoot. I couldn't think of any reason I would ever need to shoot a gun. I had decided long ago that I would simply hide if an intruder got into the house. But I went through the motions. My father also had a BB gun, and he and I had fun together trying to hit Pepsi cans from the back porch, but I had no interest in the .22 and never touched it again.

My first year in college, my father called me on the phone, drunk, to tell me he was going to kill himself. Having no one to turn to, I called the suicide prevention line.

"How can I help him?" I said.

"You can't," he replied, "but you might ask him why."

That was one of the questions I asked the woman on the phone.

The suicidal woman caller's reply did not make sense. The woman was mentally ill; my father was not.

I found a profound sense of relief in asking the woman why she wanted to kill herself. My father killed himself with a .44 Magnum, and I never got to ask him why.

After I got off the phone with the woman, my boss congratulated me. "You handled that well for your first time."

I wanted to tell her it wasn't my first time. I wanted to tell her I hadn't been so lucky in the past.

After work I went to a birthday party. The party was way out in the country and because the weather was bad not everyone who was invited showed up. As I drove down the hill toward the lake where they were, I could see them huddled in the wind. The guests were alive and eating birthday cake, and I joined them.

Descending

So I get in the elevator of memory and go down. Sometimes I get stuck between floors and am left with two visions: one known and one not. I can see the sleeping cat, a sandal left on the floor by my daughter, the sun catching a small square of linoleum. The depths are quiet and dark. I wait until the door squeezes shut. What will I find? Freedom? Wisdom? My father? Who will I be at the end of this process? Now, I can go back and take my time looking around and record what I see. Who will I be when I come back to the kitchen and my daughter and my life?

In and Out Through
a Window

1973

The first trip I took to Montana with my father was in late October in 1973. At thirteen, making the transition from life with my mother and three half siblings to life with my father was never easy. As a single parent of four children, my mother struggled to make ends meet, while my father seemed as rich as Midas. In my mother's world I was the oldest of four children in a single-parent household and had a great deal of responsibility. In my father's world I wasn't changing diapers or cooking simple meals for my little brother and sisters. My burden was emotional because I knew that my father needed me.

Up to this point, I had been able to travel back and forth between the two worlds successfully. Even though my parents had been living apart for a long time, from a cultural standpoint the two of them were very much alike. With both my parents I had learned to take the beauty of my surroundings for granted because they had always chosen exceptional places to live. San Francisco is one of the loveliest cities in the United States, and the Valley of the Moon in Sonoma County has a quiet ambiance of its own. Finally my mother decided to live surrounded by the ocean in Hawaii while my father rotated between the mountains of Montana and the city of San Francisco. I spent a great deal of time during my teenage years flying back and forth between the two households.

Although my parents had little or, in the case of my father, no contact with their families of origin, they both were attracted to older homes. My mother and father liked to speculate about people who had once lived there. When they were young neither of my parents minded the small inconveniences (like never enough hot water) that came along with older dwellings of this sort. There was rarely a lawn, or if there was one it was never mowed on a regular basis. The past was always evident, even if it was never referred to.

I remember once flipping through a 1963 *McCall's* magazine and realizing that my parents weren't represented in the pages. They didn't live in the houses, wear the clothes, cook the food, or share the values of that time. Neither of them was interested in places like Disneyland or the suburbs. Yet they never went native or pretended that we were anything but a sort of odd un-invited guest in North America, a kind of guest that had no extended family to return to or any real security, except the freedom to escape. I traveled light. I was always ready to go at a moment's notice. For years everything I owned could fit into a suitcase and a few boxes. Until my father died, I could still fit all my belongings, including a cat, into a car. Elizabeth was born almost a year from the date of his death, and so I finally had permission to settle down.

For all of my growing-up years, I longed for a traditional home. I didn't like moving. For most of my childhood I thought

I wanted to live in a house that had a kitchen with garish orange Formica counters similar to the kitchen set of *The Brady Bunch.*

What made Montana different from anywhere else I had been with my father was its sheer magnificence and the size of the mountains. We stayed at the Pine Creek Lodge, in Paradise Valley, which is just outside the town of Livingston, in a cabin next to the writers Jim Harrison and Guy de la Valdène. A clear stream ran through the property. Enchanted, I loved walking back and forth over the tiny bridge, traversing the little trail of water. I called my mother from a pay phone on the side of road. Jim Harrison gave me fly-fishing lessons. I soon figured out after a couple of long afternoons of my father worrying about me hooking myself with a fly that I wasn't a fisher person. But I did like Jim Harrison. He had a wonderful lingering kind of voice. When he finished saying a sentence, the last gravelly word re-

Pine Creek, Montana, 1998. © Ianthe Brautigan Swensen

mained hanging in the air for a while, much like a good cast. He was always trying to trick me into guessing his age. From my perspective, they all were very old. They were only in their early thirties but all of them looked terribly ancient to me. Jim thought this was funny, but I caught on and I stopped guessing.

By the age of thirteen I was skinny, very shy, and not really good at anything but reading and story-listening. The only place I could be outgoing was at the small private school I had been attending for the last three years. I often wished for special skills and talents, but I wasn't athletic, nor was I particularly adept at anything. Despite this my father was always fiercely proud of me. He told his friends that I was smart, funny, and a thinker. I was glad he thought so, but privately I felt that he was a little optimistic concerning my abilities.

One of the things that made my father unique and made me look forward to spending time with him was that almost everything concerning him centered around the story. He and his friends got together primarily to tell each other stories. And since he took me everywhere with him, I spent many hours listening to them transforming everyday events and occurrences into a kind of hard currency to be exchanged in conversation. Although one had to be extraordinarily sharp to participate in these sessions with my father and his friends, this was not a serious undertaking. They saved that kind of work for their writing. A work that had a life-or-death quality about it. A work that was the most important thing; everything else came in second, wives, children, and even the writers themselves. This fact made me sad, even then. But these stories were different. They could start out very seriously, even sadly, before transcending into something lighter and special.

An example of this is a story that the poet Lawrence Ferlinghetti told me recently. I was at an event that he was also at-tending and went up to say hello. This was to be a brief hello, since I don't know him very well. He is a very striking man, tall with blue eyes and a nice-looking beard. We exchanged greet-ings and then he leaned over a bit and said in a low tone, "I saw your father two weeks before he died." This caught my interest. I looked at him, wondering what he would say next.

"He came by City Lights, and at that time we had a display of Walt Whitman's books in the window with a bit of dried grass from Whitman's gravesite. Richard looked at it and said, 'That sure gives a good argument for cremation.'"

We parted ways, and I was left with the perfect story about my father. Not the speculative gossip about Richard Brautigan's last sad sightings in North Beach. This story was different. It kept the complexity of my father alive.

The quality of storytelling that my father's friends partici-pated in that fall when I was thirteen was truly amazing. I learned that the really good storytellers were the ones who could create stories out of nothing. I loved it when a story would start and then be added to and then bounced back to the storyteller until the story became entirely something else. The mark of superior storytellers is that they latch on to anything that sounds better and run with it. When my father would tell a story, he would usually get excited and his voice would rise in the air, leaving the last word to collapse into laughter. He rarely held still. If he was telling a story, his body movement added to the structure of the story.

Jim Harrison told his tales in a very laid-back style that I loved. Tom McGuane used his deep, dramatic voice to hold everyone. A group of good storytellers who gather together are much like the wonderful scene in the book *Mary Poppins* in which they all laugh so hard that they float up to the ceiling and decide to stay there, drinking tea five feet off the ground. When it's over, no one tries to keep it alive. Instead they sink slowly back down to the floor, somberly gather their coats, and go quietly home.

One night at the Pine Creek Lodge after a delicious meal of trout cooked by Jim Harrison and Guy de la Valdène, I went to bed in our little cabin and was lulled to sleep by the fluid sounds of their voices drifting in through the open window from where they sat nearby on old battered picnic tables. These voices and their stories changed something in me, and I went searching in my dreams for these tangible tones.

It was on that first trip, at thirteen, that I began to notice that my father drank a lot. Everyone drank, but he seemed to go one step farther. In an attempt to understand him, I got drunk for the first time on Calvados at Tom and Becky McGuane's house. In one of the bathrooms I stood spinning, holding on to the wall. Finally I threw up in the toilet and then sat down on the floor, too shaky to stand up. I could hear the laughter of my father and his friends. When I finally stepped back out into the party, nobody noticed I had been gone.

1974

My father bought a ranch about a quarter of a mile from the Pine Creek Lodge and about sixteen miles from Livingston in Paradise Valley. The following June, when I was fourteen, I flew out to spend the summer there. At that time Frontier Airlines flew into Missoula before heading on to Bozeman. I had never flown in a propjet before, let alone through a thunder-and-lightning storm over the Rocky Mountains. As the propellers buzzed and we bounced through the sky, I wondered if I would survive.

Once the plane reached Bozeman, the sky was overcast but

still. I pressed my face against the tiny airplane window, looking down at the miniature buildings and runway. My father was down there at the outside gate waiting for me, his long blond hair blowing in the wind. Seeing him, as always, gave me an overwhelming sense of joy. He was not a big hugger; instead he would pat my head and start talking as if words were the bridge between us. We got my luggage. Since my father didn't drive, someone drove us to the ranch. He loved machines, one of his nicknames for cars, but had no interest in learning to drive. We stopped in Livingston and got groceries. He showed me around, telling me about this new place I was coming to. There were an astronomical number of bars. I heard Paul Harvey on the radio, my father found him amusing, and I fell instantly in love with country-and-western music.

I was stunned by this new culture. Everything was quiet, old, straight, and the ties to the past could be plainly seen. The streets were empty compared to California. There was no problem jaywalking because there weren't very many cars. Most of the buildings were brick and were over seventy-five years old. There weren't suburbs, malls, or even a 7-Eleven.

Before we left town we stopped off at the state liquor store. In Montana you could only buy alcohol at the state liquor store and only during certain hours, and it was closed on Sundays. I had never been in a store like this one. It reminded me of an austere thrift shop. The floors were covered with a flat, gray government-issue carpet. A serious bespectacled man dressed in fifties clothes with a flattop haircut stood behind an enormous counter. The liquor stores I bought penny candy in while growing up all had linoleum floors and literally burst with dusty colorful signs advertising booze. The owners were always characters, who were used to little kids buying cigarettes and milk for their parents and penny candy with the change. This clerk looked like he had never seen a kid in his life, and he definitely wasn't in the habit of seeing someone like my dad on a regular basis. We left with gallons of white wine in pretty-shaped green bottles and a case of whiskey.

I became a little afraid of the state-owned store. It was a living monument to the dangers of excess. My father ignored all the warnings and was almost childlike picking out the alcohol. He reminded me of a kid at a fireworks stand. A part of me held my breath at the enormous quantity of liquor he bought and would continue to buy all summer long.

I could hear the bottles clinking together in the trunk. I looked out the windows at the landscape as we drove out to the ranch. Before I had been visiting Montana, but now I was going home. My father had made it clear to me that we would be spending a great deal of time at the ranch. I was going to pick out a bedroom in a house that wasn't haunted, and he was going to buy me a horse. My father had remodeled an old shed close to the house for his bedroom. This was his solution to his insomnia. He could have houseguests and not be disturbed by them.

We drove to the Tastee-Freez, where we got burgers and fries. Just beyond the Tastee-Freez was Paradise Valley. There were two highways that ran through the valley. One was the old road on the left side of the Yellowstone River and passed within a few feet of my father's front door. The new highway was on the other side of the river and was in much better condition. There was a gravel road and a wooden bridge that connected the two sides of the valley. So you could drive out on the new highway, turn at the sign for the KOA campground, and take the gravel road over to the old highway. This connector road was halfway between Pine Creek and my father's ranch. When you drove a car

My father's sleeping cabin and the ranch house, 1998. © Ianthe Brautigan Swensen

across the bridge, the wooden planks would make a noise like thunder that could be heard if you were standing outside at the ranch. Horses didn't like to cross the bridge because between the planks they could see the heavy, thick water of the Yellowstone River flowing. On sunny days the sunlight reflecting off the water seemed almost to throw sparks up in between these gaps.

As a body of water, the Yellowstone River was a disappointment to me. Although I was an excellent swimmer, it was always too dangerous and cold to swim in. That first summer I hoped that the runoff from the mountains would stop and the river would settle down, but it never did. Weekly, I rode across the fields and checked on the river, but it always looked the same. Huge and powerful. There was a beautiful creek, Pine Creek, just on the other side of the horse pasture on one side of the house. I spent time collecting stones there, and sometimes I would take a book and read under the small bridge built by the

WPA workers during the Depression. I startled one of my father's neighbors one day when he looked down, expecting to see only water, and saw me.

"I thought you were a fairy," he said.

By the time I arrived in Montana, my father had bought all the appliances for the ranch house. A washing machine, dryer, stove, and refrigerator, all seventies yellow, except for the freezer. The freezer was white. I was intrigued by this enormous appliance because it was such an odd thing for my father to have bought. The father I knew always had small apartment freezers that contained only ice cube trays and maybe, if I was lucky, a small container of ice cream. He had bought this freezer with intentions that never came to fruition, secret dreams about the ranch and the life he meant to live there.

I tried to make a dent in the freezer's vastness by buying cases of Otter pops, a sort of cheap Popsicle without a stick. I liked lifting the lid and feeling the fog of coolness touch my face and then reaching into the empty chill to grab a blue Otter pop. After that first summer, the freezer was exiled to the barn. My father realized that he was never going to buy and store large amounts of food.

Years later when I stepped into the dim, dusty interior of the barn to get my tack to go riding, I could see the freezer over in the far corner, small-looking now, covered with dust.

Even by barn standards, the barn at the ranch was huge. My father built a writing room in the very top of the barn with a window that had a breathtaking view of the Absaroka Mountains. Like all his writing rooms, I avoided it. You had to walk up a considerable amount of stairs to get to the smallish room, and once there it was clear the place was meant for one person. His new electric typewriter sat on a redwood desk. I never asked to use it. And I knew better than to interrupt him. So I rarely went up the stairs to see him. Instead I simply walked out the back door of the house, stood on the tiny footpath leading to the barn, and waved my hands up at the window, knowing that he would eventually look out. He would press his palm against the windowpane, which meant "I'll be down in a moment."

The bedroom I chose was tiny but filled with windows. I only regretted those windows once, and that was when I read Bram Stoker's *Dracula*. For a few nights after finishing the book, I worried about vampires peering in at me. Having my own room gave me hope. In the past I had had to sleep literally under his desk in his writing room, but not only was this space special, it was mine. I put the rocks I collected by the creek in jars of water, trying to keep the colors true. I did the same with fragile mountain wildflowers. In the morning when I woke up, there were huge moths on the screen doors. I took many pictures of them. Once I ran through the fields above the house with a camera, trying to get a picture of a lightning bolt. Huge lightning storms would sweep down the valley and then hover over the ranch, lighting up the yard at night and knocking out the electricity. I grew to love the smell of the coming rain as it drew near the ranch.

One morning I decided to investigate small bumping noises I had been hearing as I lay in bed mornings. The sounds seemed to be coming from the attic. I opened the door and found a nest of baby squirrels. They had no fear of me, and I played with them and then took blurry, out-of-focus pictures of them. My father was hungover, so he never saw the squirrels. As soon as I left, their nervous mother must have come and whisked them away. It was lonely in the house after the squirrels left.

There was a crow that lived in one of the cottonwood trees next to the house. She would swoop down upon us to protect her nest. The cottonwood trees let go of thousands of white tufts in June. At the end of each summer the leaves of these trees made a lovely rustling sound as the wind blew through them. I lived through a series of summers at the ranch, starting at the age of fourteen and ending when I was twenty.

The fact that my father didn't drive was always a problem in Montana. He was used to hopping on a bus to get around San Francisco. When he was young, my father hitchhiked everywhere. Back in the forties and fifties, that was an inconvenient but definitely doable form of transportation. Those days were gone. To discourage me from hitchhiking, he told me a story about how a nice rancher girl had stopped to help someone whose car had broken down and was murdered. Her fingers were found in the deranged man's pocket.

Although he developed a nice relationship with the local cab company in town, he was still, for the most part, dependent on other people for rides. He could be very charming, and usually people were willing to drive him around.

The library in town only allowed you to have either an adult card or a juvenile one. I chose the adult one, even though I hadn't yet learned to navigate the adult section of the library. My parents weren't interested in recommending books to me. Reading was an act of revolution, therefore I was expected to find my own way. Neither of them read to become well-rounded or for just the luxury of escape. Instead books gave them each a personal vision that became their road out of the limited circumstances that they had been born into. Poetry saved my father, and the Russian novelists, especially Dostoevksy, transformed the way my mother chose to live her life. She devoted her life to political activism.

I knew how to read long before I started school. My mother had taught me when I was four, the same age she had learned to read. I also read extremely fast. It was nothing for me to finish off a stack of library books over the weekend. My parents didn't care if I read the Nancy Drew or Tolstoy. Both got a similar response, silence. But I knew that behind that silence was a serious correlation concerning books and life.

Desperate for reading material, I read anything I could find at the ranch. My father didn't have a big library and had left most of his books in San Francisco. A large part of his library in the city was mimeo magazines. (They were stapled magazines that were printed on a hand-cranked mimeograph machine and handed out to friends or sold for a small sum on the street during the sixties and early seventies. They all had great names like *Sum, Change,* and *Now, Now.*) I read all of Jim Harrison's, William Hjortsberg's, and Tom McGuane's books, as well as whatever else came into the house. I even read the books that people sent to my father wanting him to review them. Some of them, like Richard Adams's *Watership Down,* I really liked. Later he bragged to his friends that I had recognized a best-seller. I read Curt Gentry's *Helter Skelter,* which, like *Dracula,* scared me to death for a few days. Late the next fall, Curt and his now ex-wife came to stay at the ranch. She could imitate the munchkins from the movie *The Wizard of Oz* and did so often, much to my delight. My father wasn't as thrilled as I was with the impersonations.

One night that first summer I tried to get my father to stop drinking by taking all the George Dickel, an expensive whiskey, and pouring it down the sink. I was home alone, and without any forethought, I started pulling quart bottles of whiskey out of the cupboard and pouring them down the kitchen sink. I worked quickly, because I knew that what I was doing wouldn't please him, and he was due home at any moment. I stopped when I had filled the kitchen with the smell of whiskey. And what happened was that my father was drinking so much that he didn't notice any absence of liquor; he just assumed he had consumed it. Soon after that night I wrote a poem in my journal about his drinking. "Daddy, when you drink beer or wine, you do just fine/but hard liquor makes you lose your mind." He kept buying George Dickel and Jack Daniel's by the case. My father was raging. My father was having blackouts. My father was suicidal. I called my mother, and she tried to understand what was happening. But by the time she talked to him in the morning he was sober, and I was already trying to forget the drunken father from the night before. The already strong division between the two worlds I lived in became complete that summer. My mother and I weren't in the habit of talking about my father, so when she did ask me questions they were easy to deflect. I also thought that everyone could see what I saw so clearly that summer—my father was in danger.

With a courage that still amazes me, I tried to talk to him about his drinking. I told him that I thought that he was drinking too much. I had been raised by a father that I could talk to about anything, but the drinking father became angry. After spending several nights listening to him in a drunken rampage, saying every hurtful thing he could think of, I realized I had made a mistake. My mother rarely raised her voice with me, and up to now my father never had either. My child's mind was completely baffled at his erratic drunken behavior. So I decided that it was my grandmother's fault. She was to blame. I thought that I looked like her and reminded him of her. Maybe that's why he was so upset with me.

"No, no, you don't look anything like her," he told me.

"Maybe I should have been a boy."

He looked surprised. "I'm glad you're not a boy. I hoped you would be a girl."

The rages continued.

One night he trapped me in the bathroom, sitting opposite me with a drink in his hand, berating me. "Just what do you think you are doing? When you are eighteen, you're on your own. Don't expect anything from me then." I remember looking at him and wondering who he was really talking to. I finally ran out of the house during a thunderstorm. I ended up sitting in the horse pasture with my arms wrapped around my knees rocking and crying. He came out into the yard calling for me. He sounded scared. I had never run away. The thunderstorm passed on the other side of the valley, and it began to rain softly. My horse found me, and I hugged her big soft neck, hiding my face in her dusty mane.

He wouldn't direct his anger at me like this again until I was twenty-one years old and wanted to get married.

But he did answer one question that I asked about his drinking that summer and that was why. We were on the back porch and the sun was setting. My father told me, while sipping white wine, that at times the type of thinking he did was so difficult that it formed steel spiderwebs in his mind and that drinking was the only way he knew how to get rid of them.

In the days that followed he told me incredibly sad stories about his childhood. He told me of growing up during the Depression, and how his mother had to move him and his sisters a great deal because of this.

"My mother had to sift the rat shit out of the flour to make water-and-flour pancakes. There were no eggs or milk."

"I had to sit outside assemblies at school with the other poor kids, because I didn't have the nickel for admittance."

"My mother left me in Great Falls alone with one of my stepfathers, who was a fry cook. I would eat meals at his place and lived in a hotel room by myself. I was seven years old."

"I watched one of my stepfathers finish cooking dinner after he had knocked my mother unconscious with a frying pan."

Some of his stepfathers had beat him as well.

He told me that as a really little kid he liked to bury the prizes that came in boxes of Cracker Jacks. One day he decided that the fact that he didn't have a nickel for a box wasn't going to get in his way. He walked into the corner store with a toy wagon and loaded it up with all the boxes of Cracker Jacks that the wagon would hold and went home. He said that he then carefully fished out all the prizes and buried them. His mother discovered what he had done. She took him back to the store, and she paid for the Cracker Jacks with the small amount of food money that she had.

"And then all we had to eat for a while was Cracker Jacks, breakfast, lunch, and dinner," he said. I think he meant this as a funny story, but my father looked so full of sorrow when he finished telling me I knew that it wasn't. I couldn't handle the fact that my father spent some of his childhood hungry. My world had been turned upside down. The only thing that became clear was that he needed much more than I did.

The object became not to upset him when he started drinking. I learned not to say anything when he showed up at my bedroom door at eight in the morning with a bar of soap in his hand telling me that this was his last will and testament. I learned how to get him to leave my bedroom when he was drunk and wanted to read me his latest short stories at three in the morning. I became savvy at getting him out of restaurants.

Sick to my stomach, watching him across the room in the murky light, turning the pages, listening to him read to me, was awful at the time. Today, I find it strangely funny. I see myself on *Sally Jessy Raphael.*

"So what terrible things did your father do to you?"

"He read to me in the middle of the night."

"What saved you?"

"The stories. They were very beautiful."

"If you weren't here," he told me one bright sunny morning, when I was fourteen, "I would have killed myself last night, but I didn't want you to find the body." As I write this, I try to feel the force of those words, but I can't. They seem to be buried deep inside of me. All I can hear is a small voice saying: Be strong. He needs you to be here and take care of him. If you fail, something terrible will happen. And so I sit here looking out over the overcast sky, which reminds me of the skies that blew by the ranch that first rainy summer of 1974, sifting through the memories of a failed past. I failed. My father is dead.

But that summer, the birds would wake me up, drawing me outside. I loved everything. The giant windows in front of the kitchen sink that gave a perfect view of the barn and of the window to my father's writing room. Even the dishwasher with its soothing whooshing sound, lulling me to sleep at night. The scent of new paint permeating the air with hopefulness. The giant cottonwood trees creaking in the slightest breeze, sending down wagonloads of white fluff that I swept into piles with the broom. My father's attorney, Richard Hodge, and his wife came to visit. He always brought out the best in my father.

We drank ice-cold water that came directly from the mountains. Pine needles clogged our faucet heads in the beginning of every summer. I was fascinated with the hand pump in the yard. It looked just like the kind they had in westerns. I would stand and crank the handle up and down until the clear water I had been warned about gushed out. I never understood why my father, who knew the difference between the bad water from the well and the good water we drank in the house, hadn't figured out what was so obvious to me: alcohol was bad for him. I pumped the water onto the ground, hoping that the sight of the poisonous water would teach me something. It never did.

Then Lexi Cowan entered our lives that first summer. My father had bought my horse from her. The horse was a gentle, mostly thoroughbred bay mare with a crooked white stripe down her nose. My father knew absolutely nothing about horses. Lexi spent hours with us as we checked the horse pasture for odd pieces of wire that could be dangerous to the horse. My father was good at that sort of thing. He found lots of wire. Lexi got in

My horse, Jackie, and me at the ranch, 1974. © Lexi Marsh

the habit of checking on the horse after she got off work. Since she came by just about the time my father started drinking, it wasn't hard to figure out that things weren't so great. None of my dad's friends showed any awareness of how bad things were. Only one, Ron Loewinsohn, a long-ago best friend of my father's, one of the many guests that first summer, remarked to me a few years ago that after staying at the ranch, he left wondering how I was going to survive.

Lexi seemed like an odd sort of angel, tall and thin with curly blond hair and blue eyes. She was gifted with extraordinary patience and wisdom beyond her twenty-one years. My father thought highly of her, yet they were never romantically involved. Her response to the situation was simple: she just tried to get me out of the house when he was drinking. She had an uncanny sense for when my dad was about to go on a binge, and before I knew it she and I'd be gone. Lexi loved to drive. She had a beautiful '66 Mustang and thought nothing of driving a hundred miles round trip to go to a dance or to the movies. Although she was only six years older than I, she spent a lot of time talking to me about how to navigate through life. She was one of the few women I had met who truly lived on her own terms. Her purse always had interesting things in it like pliers and horse-worming medicine as well as exotic colors of lipstick. All the other women I was around were caretakers of famous men. Although they were extraordinarily intelligent and kind, they didn't seem to function independently in the world. These women had no life of their own. They existed to make the life of the artist run smoothly. Yet, I often wished my father had one of these life partners.

My father was never monogamous, but he did make sure when I was younger that I saw him with the same woman for at least a couple of years. My father dated some really special women, to whom I learned not to become too attached because they would eventually disappear. When Sherry Vetter and then a few years later Siew Hwa Beh, both of whom I thought were perfect for him (and me), left, I realized that my father would never have a long-lasting relationship. Almost without exception I liked his girlfriends. Although my father told me that when I was little, I used to reduce Marcia, who is on the cover of *The Pill versus the Springhill Mine Disaster,* to tears. For a while, anytime he left me alone with Marcia, I would walk up to her and whisper, "You're not my mother—go home." He said that he would come back into the room to find Marcia understandably upset, but that he could never get really mad at me because I would just smile sweetly up at him. Despite this, Marcia was good to me.

It was one such woman who helped me in Montana. My father wanted me to be at the ranch more; he liked me to go everywhere with him. And since he led a very interesting life, I usually didn't mind accompanying him. But now Lexi was taking me to all sorts of different and fun places, riding, rodeos, even to the veterinary office where she worked. He began to object. This woman laughed at him. "Oh, Richard, she's young and doesn't want to hang around with you old farts." Twenty years later, I called her to tell her how much she meant to me. The woman was surprised. It was then I realized how much of myself I hid from those around me.

Ironically, Lexi and, much later, my stepmother, Akiko, were the only adults who ever expressed any concern about my father's drinking. I never knew how to respond, because at the time I couldn't talk about the fact that I was witnessing the father whom I worshiped, the father who was so magical, destroying himself. This destruction was fast, systematic, and very visible to me. This unnamed terror sucked up all the space around my father. I learned to quickly bury any wants or desires that conflicted with his.

Although his writer friends had problems—most of their marriages were ending dramatically—they had some sort of foundation, a class structure, families, or had successfully remarried, which enabled them to land back on their feet. My father resisted talking about his parents, though they were still living. And as I grew older, he stopped being polite about how he felt about his mother. "When you're eighteen, I'll put you on a bus and you can go visit her," he said one day. Yet it was in Montana that I began to learn bits and pieces about my father's childhood. He had only met his father twice. The picture he painted of his mother was vague and not pleasant. The only two concrete things he mentioned about her was that she drank a lot and smoked cigarettes. The poverty he described was extreme. Sitting on the porch listening to him, I got very quiet. My father became aware of this and then told me that when he was thirteen his mother married a really nice man and that this new stepfather changed their lives. This final stepfather was a kind and good man.

"He taught me how to hunt and bought me a .22 rifle for my thirteenth birthday."

My father told me that as a child, he was terrified of statues and would go blocks out of his way to avoid walking by one.

We were sitting outside on the back porch at the ranch in the early afternoon. "Why were you afraid of statues?" I asked.

"I thought they were real people that had been covered alive," he replied.

I'm haunted by the bleakness of the images that he has left

me with about his childhood. If he had survived, they might not have so much power. But because he didn't, I handle the memories as if they were pieces to a puzzle that I think might help me understand why he killed himself. As an intense, curious child, whose favorite word was "why," I wanted to know more about his childhood. This was a man who took pride in his exactness, and yet refused to name anybody from his past. His life began in 1956 in San Francisco. When I asked him where his sisters and brother lived, he looked past me, setting his gaze on the Absarokas, and replied, "I think they got married."

"But where are they?" I was extremely short on relatives. Both my grandparents on my mother's side were dead. The only other relative I had was an uncle on my mother's side, with whom I had no regular contact. I had memories of a few visits with my mother's mother before she died. And now here my father was alluding to a treasure trove of relatives, whom he refused to discuss.

"Up in the Pacific Northwest," he said finally. He wouldn't even name the state. I thought they were in Washington, because I knew that he had been born in Tacoma.

"Do they have any kids?" I persisted.

"I think one of my sisters has two kids, and my other sister married someone who was in the army."

We sat together and I waited for something. I wanted to ask him how, if he hadn't had any contact with his family since he left home at the age of twenty-one, he knew his sisters were married. He didn't say another word. I decided that if the past upset my father this much, it should be avoided at all costs.

I also learned something else that first summer, that his terror could ebb away and I could have my invincible father back. When he wasn't drinking, our days settled down. After a binge over the course of a couple of days or several weeks, he simply stopped and there were long extended periods of sobriety.

In between the stream of guests that came to visit, we were alone. He cooked us simple meals: prepackaged frozen lasagna, steaks, barbecued ribs (made in the oven). We both loved to eat. Because he was a child of the Depression, food was never taken for granted. Even the most regular food, like canned chili, was greeted with enthusiasm. "This is the best chili I've had in a while," he would tell me. After dinner we watched TV. We liked watching the farm news.

Early one of these quiet evenings, a man came to our door. His daughter had fallen off her bike on the road in front of our house. He used our phone while my father ran and got a blanket to cover her up. "Shock," my father told me. The young woman was lying on the blacktop bleeding from her ears.

"My contacts! My contacts are still in," she anxiously told my dad.

"Don't worry. Everything will be okay," he said as he carefully tucked the blanket around her. "They'll take your contacts out at the hospital."

She was loaded into the backseat of a car and driven into town because the ambulance would take too long. We called the hospital that night and found out she had been airlifted to Billings so they could operate on her brain to relieve the swelling. In the end, everything turned out all right. She was fine. This was the capable side of my father, the side good in an emergency.

One time I woke my father up in the middle of the night. My room in Montana was filled with mosquitoes. There had been a lot of rain in the spring, so the mosquitoes were really bad that year. When I went riding out in the fields the horse and I would be covered with them. That night there were just hundreds of the insects flying around the room making a high-pitched whining noise. Anytime I stuck any part of my body out from underneath the blankets, they would attack. Finally, I started crying. I went outside and knocked on my father's bedroom door. He didn't have his glasses on when he answered the door. This was a rare look for my father. Without his glasses, he couldn't see well and squinted. As a child this was a familiar look, because I usually awakened so much earlier than he. One of my earliest childhood memories is watching him walking towards me slowly putting on his glasses.

"There are too many mosquitoes in my room," I said, trying not to cry.

"Oh," he said. He came into the house and made up a bed for me in one of the guest bedrooms. Before he left, he got a flyswatter and made sure that he killed any stray mosquitoes in the new room. I got into bed, and turned out the light. I slept soundly that night.

That first summer he tried ranching. He would get a special tax deduction if he raised some animals. Since he was making a great deal of money, his accountant thought that this was a good idea. So we had four stout pigs and lots of fragile baby chicks we tried to keep alive. The chicks didn't do well, but the porkers, as my father referred to them, provided lots of entertainment. They got loose all summer. We got to know a lot of our neighbors because strangers were always knocking on the door to tell us that they had just seen our pigs galloping down the road.

One afternoon while I was out riding, my father, hearing noise in the kitchen and assuming I had come back, began telling me about his day. He had finished writing and was sitting on the couch going through his mail, and he thought that I was making a snack. Finally, when I didn't answer him, he walked into the kitchen to discover the pigs rooting around the refrigerator door. I went back to my mother's to start the ninth grade before he butchered them. He brought back some of the bacon to San Francisco, but I never ate any. I was glad when my father decided not to raise pigs again. Years later, he did, however, raise chickens, although I'm not sure he ever ate those. Those chickens became the subject of some of the stories in his book *The Tokyo–Montana Express.*

A fierce warm wind blew up from Wyoming into Montana last night and through my sleep shaking the branches of my dreams all the way down to the roots of that which I call myself.

Nightmares followed nightmares like rush hour traffic on a freeway to oblivion. . . . I cast off the chains of my last dream and my eyes tunneled out of sleep at dawn. I got out of bed quickly and dressed and went outside. I wanted to escape anything that had to do with sleep.

I was greeted by all the chickens standing outside the chicken house in a blown group staring at me. They were about thirty feet away. The wind had turned the latch on the chicken house door and then it had opened the door and there were all the chickens staring at me.

Of course when a door is open, chickens have to go out and stand in the wind. That's the way chickens think. They were lucky that they were not blown away. They would have been very surprised if they had found themselves in Idaho.

—R.B., "My Fault,"
IN *The Tokyo–Montana Express*

1975–1976

The summer I was fifteen, lots of fascinating people came to the ranch. I met more movie stars. Some, like the elegant Peter Fonda, had recently moved in down the valley. He came for dinner with his new wife, Tom McGuane's now ex-wife, Becky. Tom McGuane came with his new wife, the glamorous Margot Kidder. Of all the women that passed through that summer, Margot Kidder was one of the most intriguing. My father adored Becky, but he refused to talk about all the couple shuffling that was going on. "If I tried to keep track of the substance of my friends' love lives, that's all I would have time to do," he told me wearily one afternoon when I tried to press him for answers. He was very fatalistic about love.

Margot was captivating. I don't believe she ever spoke more than one word to me, but I loved to watch her. She couldn't cook, never washed the dishes, and wasn't quiet. She was not a writer's wife.

Drugs were everywhere, although I remained very protected. My father didn't do coke or smoke pot. He drank and occasionally took Valium in order to sleep. Although drinking was the norm, and I drank openly in front of adults, I was never offered as much as a hit off a joint. The exception was at a party at our neighbors' when I became curious about why the majority of the adults were so high. I found out that they were dropping acid. I remember wanting to drop acid too and I even found someone who was willing to give me a hit. Suddenly one of the hosts of the party found out, and the offer was instantly withdrawn.

In the middle of all this, it was decided that I would stay on with my father and spend the school year in Montana with him. Terry de la Valdène registered me for school and took me clothes shopping. She also had taken over the organization of the kitchen while she was visiting the ranch with her husband. During the long evenings Terry and I would wash the endless dishes together while she told me funny stories about growing up. I was sad when she left.

Fortunately, Tony Dingman, a poet, arrived at the ranch. He provided a kind of stability to the ranch that no one else really could. He never complained when I played Bob Marley over and over again and was one of the few people who could get along with my father for long periods of time. I always felt very safe when Tony came to stay with us. He solved the transportation problem because he could drive, and he convinced my dad to buy a used car, which my father christened the White Acre because of its color and size.

If my father drank too much, Tony took care of him. The two of them liked to play practical jokes on me. And they had the advantage of having the entire school day to plan things. That summer practical jokes had been big with my dad's friends. One cool summer evening, knowing that Jim Harrison was tired and planning to leave a dinner party at our next-door neighbors', the Hjortsbergs, early and come back to the guest room at the ranch and go to sleep, my father slipped home and created another guest in Jim's bed. The guest had a coconut for a head and pillows for a body. Much to my father's delight, Jim came back to the party. He was bewildered but polite, not asking whom my father had displaced him with. Eventually my father confessed, and Jim was able to go to bed. He retaliated a couple of nights later by slathering butter on the doorknob to my dad's bedroom. My father was very drunk and was unable to open his door without coming back into the kitchen to wash his hands and get a dish towel.

One day I came home from school and was considerably put out because my father and a friend had eaten the last of the chocolate chip cookies I had baked. A couple of days later, I discovered that they had hidden chocolate chip cookies everywhere in my room. They were under my pillow, in my shoes, in my desk. I found cookies for weeks.

The jokes culminated in a giant food fight one night after dinner. I woke up the next morning to the sound of the lawn sprinkler. Looking out the window, I saw the sprinkler going slowly back and forth over our living-room rug lying on the front lawn, which, after it dried out, was fine. The kitchen walls were so stained that they had to be repainted along with the living-room ceiling. Tony left a little square of yellow on the wall in the kitchen that had my height marks on it.

Finally all the people were gone. I think my father was relieved. We waited for it to snow. These were the good times, the times in which my father was relaxed. We went to quiet dinners at people's houses and rode over to Bozeman to go to the movies. During the day he worked in his writing room and then liked to check the mail and wait by the mailbox for my school bus to come rattling down the old highway.

I rarely spoke to anyone on the bus. Our driver was a big, tall rancher who drove the school bus to make extra money in the winter. I used to lay my cheek against the window and try to sleep in between the jolts from the potholes in the road.

I know that I hurt my father's feelings a little when I suggested to him that fathers didn't meet the school buses of teenagers. I enjoyed going to the high school in Livingston. My father asked me a few questions about what I studied. He was puzzled when I showed him the reading list of my contemporary novel class. "I didn't realize Huxley was considered contemporary," he said. And when I complained about how boring I thought Faulkner's short story "The Bear" was, he looked alarmed and said that he didn't know why a teacher would give that to a teenager to read and instead gave me the novel *As I Lay Dying.* He loved Faulkner and wanted to make sure that I was introduced to this writer properly.

Then the temperature dropped and it snowed.

Just before Halloween, my father decided to leave Montana. I still don't know why. Another part of my world collapsed. There was not any advance warning. In a journal that he kept from January to November 1975, he wrote that he planned on staying in Montana until the spring: "Ianthe and I went and got some bulbs for planting. I want some daffodils in the spring." And yet a previous day's entry reads, "I went and burned all the telephones in the house in the fireplace. They burn with a sharp flame."

My father's relationship to the telephone was rather extraordinary. Before anyone thought about it, he had a switch put on his phone that enabled him to turn it off. He purchased one of the first answering machines. He had long cords, enabling him to walk throughout the house, two fingers hooked under the receiver, talking and laughing. When we were apart, he and I talked on the telephone a lot. I learned to call him collect long before I learned to ride a bike. I would call him person-to-person and then he would call me right back. He liked to talk to me on the phone and often told me funny stories. Once he called laughing to say that he had called a friend and had launched into a story and when he finished the story, an unfamiliar voice said to him, "I don't know who the hell you are, but that was a very funny story."

I slept through the night he burned the phones. The next morning I woke up smelling gas. I could tell by a particular silence in the house that people had been drinking all night. I went to call the gas company to find out what the smell was but couldn't find the phones. I looked everywhere. All I found was glasses with watery whiskey in them. I knew my father wouldn't have moved the phones out to his bedroom, the remodeled shed, because he had a phone out there. I looked harder. Finally, I noticed a nest of odd wires in the fireplace. I knelt down and put my hands in the soft silver ashes and pulled out a small amount of foreign material. I sat back on my heels. He had burned the phones. A tiny snarl of wires, that was all that was left of the baby-blue princess phones. I straightened up and opened all the windows to try to dissipate the smell of gas, put on my coat because it was cold, and waited until someone woke up.

The ladies at Mountain Bell were not happy.

"They want to know what happened with my phones. I can't tell them I burned them, can I?" my father asked. He tried to get Tony Dingman to ask for replacements. Tony just laughed at him. And so it was my father who strode into the Mountain Bell office and came out with two new phones. The cleaning woman came and straightened up. The new phones looked just like the old phones.

I inherited all my father's surviving phones. I have black ones, blue ones, and white ones. I wish I had the phone that he was holding on the album cover for a record he made. If you look carefully at that phone, you can see the turn-off device. *Listening to Richard Brautigan* was the title of the album he made with Harvest Records. He had me read "Love Poem," from *The Pill Versus the Springhill Mine Disaster,* when I was eight years old, along with some famous friends.

He paid me eleven dollars, and I spent every cent on Cracker Jacks and Archie comic books.

One half of the album cover was a picture of him standing in his Geary Street apartment, holding a black phone to his ear. The other half showed his girlfriend Valerie looking up at the ceiling, waiting for someone to call. I thought Valerie looked like my mother. They both had beautiful long brown hair.

Printed on the record cover in black letters was a biography of my father, the last sentence of which states, "His telephone number is 567-3389." So many people called him that he had to change the number. This was a shock to my father. I don't think he actually thought that people would call him. This overwhelming response and, a few months later, someone hollowing out a book of his, placing feces in it, and mailing it to him ended any innocence he had about his fame.

This was the cycle of our lives, dark, lonely despair one day and the hope of daffodils planted for a future in the next. My life was woven in the fabric of his and there were not many boundaries, yet the extraordinary quality of this hope is why I'm still alive. In his own life, as well as in his writing, he could expand a moment in time. My father's almost Zenlike ability to inhabit fractions of time was one of the things that made him truly amazing. When he was present all was well, and when he wasn't I endured. My love for him was so strong I tolerated the unbearable. I made up reasons for his leaving. Now from what I can make out from this journal, which is only the slimmest of records of this period of time in his life, he was trying desperately to find a reason to live. Although hardcover sales were good, the reviews of his latest book, *Willard and His Bowling Trophies,* were brutal. A reviewer from the *Saturday Review* wrote, *Willard* is the "worst novel" of 1975. I didn't read *Willard* until I was a senior in high school. His form of censorship was to keep all the copies of *Willard* either in his bedroom or in his writing room, two places I rarely went.

"You can read it when you're eighteen."

The last entry in his journal is six days after he left me with Lexi and reads:

> I'm trying to get my shit together here in San Francisco
> i.e. the rest of my life.

> It is a very warm
> and nice day.

Fortunately, before my father had departed Montana in the fall of 1975, Lexi and her sister, Deane, stepped in and offered to take care of me for the rest of the school year. My mother had just moved from California to Hawaii, and I couldn't imagine starting what would be my eleventh school. I was exhausted, and I didn't want to leave. Also I was holding out, so sure he would return. He had left Montana before for quick trips to San Francisco and to go hunting, but he always came back.

My father set up charge accounts for me at Sax & Fryer's, a book and camera store, owned by a friend, John Fryer, and at clothing shops. He also opened up a bank account for me and told me that he would be sending me money every month.

I don't remember moving to Lexi's. All I took with me was a suitcase and a little cat named Mittens, whom I had adopted against my father's wishes. I had gotten her into the house and past my father's objections by convincing him that it was temporary and that the ranch was her only sanctuary from death. I left everything else at the ranch, including my memory of saying good-bye to my father.

What I do remember about that time takes place a few weeks later on a cold glittering day after a foot of snow had fallen. I needed to get my horse from the ranch to Deane's. Deane owned a little place across the creek from Lexi's where I was going to pasture my horse for the winter.

The ranch was empty and lonely without my father. In the front yard Lexi zipped up my insulated coveralls, pulled a huge knit hat over my head, wrapped a muffler around my neck, and gave me a boost into the saddle. I could tell that she was tempted to follow me by car all the way to her place, but she resisted this temptation. She finally said firmly, "Deane is making us lunch. So keep up a good pace: trot, walk, trot, walk, and you'll be at Mill Creek around noon. If you don't arrive at noon, I'll be back to find you."

At about the halfway mark my horse lost her footing on some ice, and I fell with a soft *plop* into the snow. I lay there for a moment with the snow nestling me like feathers looking up at the blue perfect Montana sky. Finally my horse looked down at me with her brown eyes and gave me a little nudge with her soft warm nose. I got back on and continued on my way.

I didn't see my father until after Christmas on my way back from Hawaii, where I had been visiting my mother and half brother and sisters over the holiday break. I stayed with him for an extra week in San Francisco because I had come down with bronchitis and was too sick to travel on to Montana. I knew that things had gotten worse, because he walked me from Coit Tower across from where his apartment was to the other side of Columbus to see the doctor and didn't stay to see what was wrong with me. He hadn't given me enough money for both a cab and the prescription for antibiotics, so I had to decide whether to walk back, running a fever of 102, and buy the antibiotics or take a cab home. After I filled the prescription, I walked back to his place, too tired and sick to cry. I was fifteen but I felt like an old, old woman whose life was coming to an end.

When I asked him what was going to happen to me, he told me that I could go to Japan with him and go to a boarding school there or I could go to Hawaii to be with my mother. Neither of the choices seemed good to me. During that visit, my father was also breaking up with his girlfriend, waiting for his visa to come through, and drinking nonstop.

With the money he handed me by the fistful, I ordered takeout and managed to keep things together until I was well enough to fly back to Montana. The only exception was when I needed to write a paper for my biology class during my stay in San Francisco. He took the time to make sure I had all the supplies I needed and let me use his typewriter and his writing room without any cautionary remarks. That access and freedom to his private space was a valuable gift for a teenage girl. Even though I was sick, the power of sitting in his writing room for hours at a time was intoxicating. My father was wounded, but I found a place where his magic, miraculously, was untouched.

He left for Japan and didn't come back to Montana for seven months. I stayed with Lexi and Deane. They tried to pick up the pieces and saved me in a hundred perfectly ordinary ways.

1976–1977

Those tears had to come from someplace, so it might as well be from hidden crying springs that came from deep in the earth and flowed great distances, originating at cemeteries and from cheap hotel rooms decorated in loneliness and despair.

Unfortunately, there is enough grief around to irrigate the Sahara.

—R.B., *Sombrero Fallout*

While my father was in Japan, my horse had to be destroyed because of a broken leg. Dr. Colmey put her down and afterwards I sat with her head in my lap, stroking her neck and looking across the field where I could see the shingled roof of the ranch house. The grass leaned horizontally with the wind. I could see the barn and the window of the writing room where my father would disappear. He would come down and announce whether or not he had had a good day. Once I asked him what a good day was. He looked at me curiously and replied, "Eight pages. Sixteen pages is even better."

But now he wasn't there; he was in Japan. He wasn't coming home until the end of July.

The ranchers who owned the adjacent fields came by and told us that they had a backhoe and would bury the horse. Deane and Lexi drove me back to Mill Creek. They had entered me in the local Rodeo Queen Contest, and now since my horse had died I was forced to ride a flashy palomino of Deane's. He was a bit of a character in that he liked to catch his riders off guard and either buck them off or run away with them. I wasn't any match for him. The judges of the contest were confused about how I ended up in the state of Montana without either of my parents.

When my father finally did come back I knew the truth: he couldn't take care of me. The ranch was an illusion. My bedroom was false. Anything he gave me would be taken away. When I think about what I would have settled for, did settle for, it was very sad. The ranch held the glimpse of a life that never came to be. There had been the potential for a small future. All the props were there for taking care of a kid: dishes and food and space and nice things like horses and breakfast cereal and music, but not my dad. He just couldn't manage it. Reading a day-to-day accounting of his life which he kept in 1975, that previous fall, helps in understanding how tormented he was. In this journal he keeps a numbered track of his days similar in some respects to the character Cameron in *The Hawkline Monster*:

> *Cameron was a counter. He vomited nineteen times to San Francisco. He liked to count everything that he did. This made Greer a little nervous when he first met up with Cameron years ago, but he'd gotten used to it by now. He had to or it might have driven him crazy.*

My father records what he ate for breakfast:

Saturday, August 30, 1975
(2) I had a hamburger with some grapefruit juice for breakfast.

Thursday, September 4, 1975
(1) I ate hot dogs and beans for breakfast at 2:00 p.m. because I stayed up drinking until 4:00 a.m.

My father records what he was writing:

Monday, September 1, 1975
(1) I typed 8 pages on my new novel.

Friday, September 26, 1975
(4) I worked on my novel.

Wednesday, October 8, 1975
(2) I copy-edited the manuscript of *Loading Mercury with a Pitchfork.* It didn't look bad.

Sunday, October 19, 1975
(3) I worked on my novel. It's getting there.

Thursday, October 23, 1975
(1) I worked on my novel all day, proofreading it etc. novel in beautiful shape. . . .

Visits with friends:

Saturday, August 30, 1975
(5) I had dinner at Russ Chatham's place on Deep Creek.

Monday, September 22, 1975
(2) I went up to Tom McGuane's and had some coffee with him. . . . We talked about W. B. Yeats.

Tuesday, September 23, 1975
(3) I went over and visited with Gatz.

Wednesday, September 24, 1975
(5) I went over to Becky's place and I had a nice conversation with her.

Fishing:

> Sunday, August 31, 1975
> (4) I went fishing on the west fork of Mill Creek and caught a cutthroat trout that weighed a pound.

> Wednesday, September 3, 1975
> (5) I went fishing on Nelson Spring Creek. It was a very beautiful autumn day but the fishing was very slow. I caught one.

> Saturday, September 27, 1975
> (3) I went fishing with Stuart on Nelson Spring Creek and caught 4 trout, including a 20-incher.

And he records his drinking, and then how disappointed in himself he was and how little control he had over it:

> Friday September 19, 1975
> (1) I woke up with a terrible hangover.

> Tuesday, September 23, 1975
> (3) I woke up with a hangover.

> Wednesday, September 24, 1975
> (7) I got very drunk again. It was not a good idea.

> Thursday, September 25, 1975
> (4) I woke up with a hideous hangover. . . .

> Saturday, October 11, 1975
> (4) I went back to bed and spent almost the whole day there. It seemed like the best place for me. I got up around dark and made jokes about being a vampire.

> Sunday, October 12, 1975

(4) I drank too much again am disappointed in myself by doing so.

Wednesday, October 15, 1975
(6) I had another hangover what's new?

Monday, October 20, 1975
(7) I didn't drink today.

Wednesday, October 22, 1975
(2) I'm not drinking at all.

Thursday, October 30, 1975
(2) I started drinking
(3) I didn't stop
(4) I ended up drinking half a dozen shots. No good came of it.

Yet, there was so much about that time that was good. To be honest, I didn't realize how much he was drinking during that time. One could imagine that I had an optimistic view of things, except I remember the burning of the phones (which he notes in his journal). The quality of the person that my father was is shown in this brief accounting of his life. He was drinking and lost entire days to hangovers. Yet during this period of time, he was editing *Loading Mercury with a Pitchfork,* dealing with bad reviews of *Willard,* spending time with his girlfriend, writing a new novel, going on short trips, fishing, visiting with friends, doing business, and being a father.

Saturday, August 30, 1975
(4) The horses came down to the end of the pasture, Jackie had a small cut on her forehead, but it didn't look serious.

Tuesday, September 2, 1975
(4) My daughter and I talked about the FBI.

Friday, September 19, 1975
(4) I had a pleasant time with my daughter.

Sunday, September 21, 1975
(5) I had a long and very rewarding conversation with my daughter.

Friday, September 26, 1975
(1) We drove over to Bozeman to take my daughter to the dentist. She was in a very chatty mood.
(5) I went for a walk with my daughter down into the big fields, and I had a long talk with her.

Thursday, October 16, 1975
(2) I bought a waffle iron for Ianthe, she's wanted one for a long time.

Saturday, October 25, 1975
(3) Ianthe and I went into town and got some bulbs for planting. I want some daffodils in the spring.

Wednesday, October 29, 1975
(2) . . . going: away.

The following summer, in 1976, to try to make up for his seven-month absence, my father flew my friend Cadence up to the ranch. A driver met her at the airport. My father sat in the backseat and was incredibly funny and charming. He called Cadence "Shirley," her mother's name, and then corrected himself. But Cadence said in the days that followed he seemed to her to be "autocratic and self-centered and arbitrary. It obviously affected you a lot. I don't know if that's how you remember it, but you were very vulnerable to his whims and demands and ever vigilant to making the necessary adjustments. I remember you loved him, but you had a sort of grim (or maybe just stoic) resolve to keep your head above water. You never cried or complained about any of it to me."

Cadence was defiant towards my father. I remember being afraid of her willingness to stand up against him. He got mad at Cadence and me for playing a practical joke on him—while he was up in his writing room, we set all the clocks in the house back an hour. She refused to apologize. "He's blowing this way out of proportion" was her final comment on the incident.

Other people came to the ranch, a strange woman whom my father was sleeping with and a longtime friend of his. This was the very same one who shot out the clock in the kitchen with my father.

One night at about one in the morning, I woke up to the sound of furniture being smashed. I whispered Cadence's name. Her eyes flew open in the dark. We both listened together. My father was breaking everything he could in the living room, which was very close to where we were sleeping. For the first time I was truly scared.

"Let's get out of here," she whispered. We fled shoeless into the bathroom and crawled out through the small bathroom window. Barefoot, we ran over to our neighbors, who were away on a trip. But some nice hippies who were house-sitting for them were still up and let us use the phone. No one asked us why. Lexi's sister, Deane, came to get us. We woke up the next morning and my father's friend and the woman, who was at the center of the night's drama, came by. My father's friend, whom I had known all my life and who was the funniest storyteller of all, was leaving. "I just wanted you to know that we are split-

*Bathroom window at
the ranch.*
© Ianthe Brautigan Swensen

ting. Things are just too crazy here." He had locked his keys in
the trunk and then broken into the brand-new rental car with a
screwdriver.

Around noon, Lexi took us back to the ranch. My father, who
had had a blackout, never acknowledged that we had ever even
left. He had swept up all the broken glass and put broken furniture in the attic. Then my father wasn't drinking and the good
father came back. For the rest of the visit he and Cadence got
along really well. He made Cadence and me laugh by appearing
in the morning in his huge Japanese kimono wearing cowboy
boots. He performed little made-up dance routines for us,
singing off-key, pretending to tap-dance, flapping around the
kitchen until Cadence and I were laughing so hard that we made
him laugh. He appreciated Cadence's intelligence.

"I remember talking to your dad about how he decided the
order and layout of a book of poems or short stories. He was so
articulate and precise in the way he explained things. One of the
great things about your dad was that he was never condescend-

ing when he talked to us. I had the sense that he was over-whelmed with dealing with interviewers who wanted to talk to him about his latest book, *Sombrero Fallout.* He said that jour-nalists asked him weird questions that left him puzzled."

Cadence and I drank mocha-flavored instant coffee. We ar-gued about the economic plight of the ranchers. Cadence neu-tralized the horror of country with Joni Mitchell's album *Court and Spark,* as well as other records she had carefully packed. She banned country-and-western music for the duration of her stay. The only exception was Dolly Parton's twangy "Jolene" that my father liked to play over and over again.

"Man alive, your dad loved that song."

"What do you think I was getting away from when I crawled out of the bedroom window?" I asked Cadence later.

"Death," she said. "I think you were crawling away from death."

At the end of that summer in 1976, I left for Hawaii, and I spent my junior year of high school there. It was the twelfth school that I attended. I was a stripped-down version of myself in the middle of a war that I was losing. I flew back and forth from Hawaii to San Francisco during the fall and early winter to visit my father before he left for the Far East again. In the spring, my father wanted me to join him in Japan, so the day af-ter my seventeenth birthday I did.

Japan

During spring vacation, half the high school in Hawaii burned down while I was visiting my father in Japan, so I stayed an extra week in my room on the twenty-sixth floor of the Keio Plaza Hotel. My father lived in a suite on the thirty-fifth floor. This distance in proximity reflected the reality of the relationship. I rarely went up there. Instead, we communicated on the phone. He called me up to get my order. We were going to eat breakfast in his suite.

"Poached eggs and toast."

"That's a safe choice," he said.

When I walked into his rooms, I was surprised to find them dim. He had the curtains closed with just a tiny crack opened to let in a little light. Although it was a nice suite, done up in neutral colors, it seemed absent of my father. I wasn't sure why he was spending so much time in Japan, except that I knew that he liked to write there. He had completed a book of poetry, *June 30th, June 30th,* during his previous stay. I was curious to see for myself where it was that he had disappeared to in 1976.

He apologized for that fact that there wasn't a swimming pool in the hotel, but he arranged for a pass so that I could swim at a health club nearby. This was the father who knew that I loved to swim and tried to make sure that when I traveled with him there was a swimming pool where we stayed. Once on a trip to Santa Fe when I was twelve, he and I were both disappointed because we found out after checking in that the tiled pool that this particular hotel was so famous for was being renovated. It turned out not to matter, because I came down with strep throat. After my father took me to the doctor and filled my prescription, I spent most of my time sleeping, ordering orange juice from room service, and reading comics.

Quite by accident, I ended my short-lived attraction to Valium in Japan. Before I left Hawaii, I had been taking about sixty milligrams a day for no better reason than that a friend had come by a large bottle of them. The night I arrived, my father offered me half of a five-milligram Valium "for jet lag," he said. I watched as he carefully cut it in half. I almost laughed out loud and refused it. I wasn't sure I would feel the effect of only two and a half milligrams.

We were a strange pair that trip. I was depressed, coming down off Valium, and he was on a drinking jag.

Tokyo was dreary in the daytime, empty. Since my father was on a nighttime schedule, I was alone. During the day, I swam at the health club and explored the enormous Keio Plaza Hotel.

Despite all the alcohol, he planned a great many things for us to do. He wanted me to like Japan and gave me the Brautigan tour: the plastic food in the windows of the noodle shops, pachinko machines, cherry blossoms at midnight, the bullet train, and Kyoto.

The second night we went out and wandered through Tokyo with its multicolored neon lights shining down on us like bright stars. We went to the Tokyo equivalent of Times Square. All the marquees seemed to be advertising Barbra Streisand's movie *A Star Is Born*. My father was excited and playful, making jokes and laughing. He teased me because I had won a pair of socks playing pachinko and then had to carry the socks around with me for the rest of the night. We ate at a restaurant that had low tables with little benches to sit on, and they served an entire grouper lined with sushi. He coached me beforehand, making sure I knew how to put my chopsticks properly on the bowl.

"Never put them this way; it means death."

Luckily, I liked sushi, because that was pretty much all we ate. The only place I could get American food and forks was at the Keio Plaza. Most nights we went to restaurants. He liked sitting around drinking until two or three in the morning. I drank screwdrivers, because it was the only drink I knew how to order. I didn't try to keep track of what he drank anymore; I had learned firsthand that alcohol could cut my pain.

The people we were with were writers and artists, and I was too shy to add to the conversation. So I half listened to the different conversations, which were always stopping and starting according to the amount of clarification that was needed in order to bridge English and Japanese. The Cradle was a fascinating bar, a gathering place for artists in Tokyo, but by the time we arrived there I was so tired that I could hardly keep my eyes open. Shiina Takako, the owner and a good friend of my father's, noticed this and found a small couch for me to lie down on.

My father had timed my visit to coincide with the cherry blossom festival. We walked around at midnight, watching

My father and me in Japan, 1977.

people singing karaoke on green lawns beneath a ceiling of pink branches.

One night we went by cab to different parts of Tokyo. I saw my first experimental theater. I remember that they were eating a lot of cabbage onstage. It was odd but interesting for a teenager. Another night I met my future stepmother, a spectacularly beautiful woman, Akiko. My father had emphasized to me that the relationship was important. She had a small white car, and as is the custom she gave me a gift, little paper birds.

In Kyoto I discovered temples. You can make wishes at them.

"Ianthe made a wish at every temple we walked by," he told his friends later. He never asked what I was wishing so hard for, and I never noticed he was watching. We spent a long, quiet afternoon at the Moss Temple. I kept a dog-eared poster I bought there for years to remind me of crouching down beside my father to look at the waterfall stones.

My father finally convinced me that the signs in one of the parks we picnicked at really did say WATCH OUT FOR MONKEYS. Even so, I still had a hard time believing that there were wild monkeys on the loose.

I figured out that if I wanted to get back to the hotel before dawn, I had to gauge his drinking and suggest the idea of going home before he went down the river of new ideas for the extremely drunk.

We didn't go to Mount Fuji as planned because he was too hungover, but the next day we took the bullet train and watched a TV series being filmed. An actress in traditional Japanese dress entered the scene and needed to light a lantern. They kept having to shoot the scene over and over because the lantern refused to light. Finally, a stagehand crouched down out of sight and was able to light it when she came near.

My father bought me a beautiful watch on a gold chain. It was an unusual gift from him because it was a surprise. This watch meant a lot to me because he thought up the idea himself. Most gifts he gave me were things that he knew I wanted.

The streets were clean but the same color gray as the sky. I'm still not sure why he drank so much then. He had just started dating my future stepmother. He should have been happy. He wasn't.

Right before I left Japan, two 747s collided on a runway in the Canary Islands, killing more than a hundred passengers. And since the only magazines I could find in English were news magazines, the photo images of the mangled people kept popping to mind as I flew alone through the turbulence on my return trip. I tried to sleep lying across three seats. I folded my arms tightly across my chest while the flight attendant buckled me around the waist and feet to keep me from falling to the floor.

1977–1978

My fourth and final summer in Montana, I felt forsaken. The horse was dead. My father married a woman I had only met once while I was visiting him in Japan. Akiko seemed very nice, but I didn't know her.

Once back in Hawaii, I continued taking drugs my senior year until I realized that I was going to die if I kept on doing what I was doing. I graduated from high school in Hawaii and went back to Montana to stay. Deane and Lexi helped me get a job at Chico Hot Springs, a well-known resort in Paradise Valley up the road from Pine Creek. My father was in Japan, having left Akiko in San Francisco. I felt sorry for her because she didn't know very many people in the city, and I knew what it was like to be left by my father. She couldn't travel with him because of residency requirements.

I was so scared, convinced that I wouldn't be able to handle the small responsibilities of being a desk clerk. To my surprise, I was able to keep the job. This gave me the confidence to apply to college in California.

1979

When it was time for me to start school, my father had returned to California and was living in San Francisco. Akiko had a stabilizing influence on him for a time, and he was able to reach out to me and help me plan the move. I enrolled in college and stayed with them in San Francisco for a few months until I moved out to the house in Bolinas. The Bolinas house was sitting empty and was only about a half-hour commute over Mount Tamalpais to the college I was attending. I made an uneasy truce with the house and ghost.

Many intriguing people were popping in and out of my father's life. We went to Francis Ford Coppola's house and watched a screening of *Apocalypse Now.* He and his friends liked to have brunch at the Washington Square Bar & Grill, and I loved listening to the sober breakfast talk. I witnessed a hysterical evening with Dennis Hopper and my father at his apartment on Russian Hill. When I went to bed they were still drinking, and since my father loved to listen to Dennis recite the soliloquy from Hamlet there were snippets of Shakespeare echoing around the apartment until the wee hours. By the time I woke up, my stepmother, who was furious at them for staying up all night, was gone. My father was sleeping, but Dennis Hopper was in the kitchen, thirsty, looking for anything alcoholic. He enlisted my help, but they had been thorough the night before. All I could find was a bottle of Chinese liqueur with a small pickled lizard lying in the bottom. I'll never forget my classy stepmother's response to seeing Hopper still in the apartment: "Shit! Shit! Shit!" I had never heard her swear.

Soon after this, Akiko sat down across from me at the kitchen table to try to talk to me about my father's problems with alcohol, but like any good child of someone who drinks to excess, I was of no help. From my perspective, things seemed so much better since he had married her. And although I never really got to know her very well, Akiko was always kind to me and I knew that she loved my father.

1980

My father and Akiko had split up. I never even got to say good-bye to her. He left for Montana as soon as the divorce was close to being final. The divorce sobered my father up a bit and left him cash-poor. He wanted me to join him in Montana in the early fall. I went back to the ranch one last time. He was getting ready to go on a huge book tour for *The Tokyo–Montana Express,* and I was going to move to New York to go to acting school. When I arrived in Montana, I learned that Lexi had gotten married to a sweet man who appeared to love horses almost as much as she did. Our neighbors, the Hjortsbergs, had gotten divorced, and my father and Marion Hjortsberg had become close friends. I got my old desk clerk job back at Chico Hot Springs. My father wasn't binge drinking. Still, returning to the ranch after the late shift at Chico, I never knew what I would find. One such night I was sitting in the quiet kitchen eating some noodles when a small, well-dressed man knocked on the back door. He had been making a phone call out in my dad's bedroom and while he was doing this, he explained, everyone had left for McGuane's ranch in Deep Creek eight miles away.

I didn't quite know what to do with him, so I offered to drive him up there. The man turned out to be someone very famous. He wasn't used to being forgotten. I didn't go in to the party at McGuane's. Instead I sat in the car and watched them through the window. In an odd way I had a sort of unrequited love for these glamorous people who didn't know me but changed who I was. I felt as though they and my father had been a sort of traveling carnival. But now it was fall, and not everyone had survived the gaiety. The leaves were turning and being pushed across the ground, making a hollow rattling sound.

My father had a new girlfriend, who was sweet but the same age that I was. He was drinking heavily again, but he didn't get angry at me if I commented on his behavior.

One night he tried to leave a saloon with a glass of whiskey in his hand. When the young waitress tried to stop him, he turned, looked her in the eye, and slowly let go of the glass, which shattered on the floor.

"I guess there isn't a problem now, is there."

She looked as though she were going to burst into tears. I refused to speak to him on the ride home. The next morning I woke up to him whispering outside my closed door. "I'm not a guard at Auschwitz. Have pity on your poor old dad."

The morning sun was pouring onto my bedroom floor. He had a cup of instant coffee ready for me in the kitchen. My father was hopeful about his impending book tour and the book. This was the first tour he had agreed to go on in years.

Late one afternoon before we left, I drove him up to Peg Allen's ranch to fish. My father disappeared up a narrow creek to catch some trout for dinner. I sat alone for about an hour until the sun had set and the mosquitoes had risen off the water and were biting me. He reappeared just as silently as he had vanished. A pickup truck stopped on the road above us. The rancher craned his neck out of the pickup window and shouted down to my father.

"How's the fishing up there?"

My father looked sorrowful and shook his head. "Terrible," he answered. "Didn't catch a thing."

"Well, better luck next time."

My father loaded up his gear while I worried how I was going to turn around on the narrow gravel road. Once we were heading back down the mountain, I told him I was sorry we weren't having trout for dinner.

"Who said we weren't having fish for supper?" he said, surprised.

"You did," I answered. "Back there to that rancher."

"Oh, that. No. No. I caught my limit."

I shook my head in mock disapproval as he cackled to himself.

Back at the ranch I made a small salad and he fried up the trout. We sat enjoying each other's company in the warm kitchen ablaze with so much light that it spilled out into that dark fall evening.

I closed up the ranch with him, putting antifreeze in the toilets, not knowing that would be the last time we would be there together. American critics hated the book *The Tokyo–Montana Express,* and his next book, a small masterpiece, *So the Wind Won't Blow It All Away.* His writing had only gotten better, but times had changed, and during the wave of conservatism that had swept the eighties, people were distancing themselves from the sixties and confused this time with my father's writing. And most critics didn't understand him, because he was always on the forefront of literary exploration.

The ranch was sold after his death to cover his debts.

One night I dreamed that I walked into an old house and went into the bathroom, opened the medicine cabinet, and found to my surprise that I could see the state of Montana behind the glass shelves. I carefully removed the shelves and climbed up on the sink and crawled back into Montana. I entered the state on the top of a tall ridge overlooking Paradise Valley. My view was unmarred by telephone lines or roads. This is really a big place, I said to myself. I had forgotten how enormous Montana really is. I woke up in the early morning and remembered riding endlessly up into the mountains to discover small streams and what it felt like to lie on the lawn on a crisp black night watching the millions of stars. I also remembered that this was the place where my father began to die.

Wrestling in the Snow

I stood outside by the car in the dark with only a bit of moon and a porch light to reflect off the snow while my father and the friend wrestled in the snow. The endless snowflakes that my father pitted himself against were soft. I knew that he couldn't hurt himself wrestling with snow and that the friend he was wrestling with would never hurt my father. Over and over they rolled in the snow as I watched embarrassed, wishing they would stop. But a part of me remained curious. Who was my father wrestling with? It was obvious even then that his friend was standing for something, someone. My father told me that during the Depression he and his sister were boarded out to a family for a while. She was beaten every morning for wetting the bed. One of his drunken stepfathers came to visit and wrestled with him, almost breaking my father's arm. Luckily, the people he was boarding with stepped in and stopped the stepfather. Now I sit, watching myself at fifteen and then twenty-one, and now thirty-six, observing my father, recreating this memory. He left me a clue under the moon on a soft blanket of snow.

What I Look Like

I have lots of baby pictures and pictures of my parents. The two of them were exotic. They took me backpacking when I was six weeks old. There is a photograph of me in a papoose board. They captured each other in offbeat poses that set them apart from previous generations. After their separation, the pictures stopped. My father didn't own a camera again for fourteen years.

When I was eight years old my father put me on the cover of a compendium of *Trout Fishing in America, In Watermelon Sugar,* and *The Pill Versus the Springhill Mine Disaster.* An all-day shoot. Nickie was on the cover too. She was the girlfriend of one of his friends and had been on the cover of *Trout Fishing in America.* I remember her skin, the color of cream. I don't know why he chose her, except that she was very unusual-looking. A special dress was made for me by my dad's girlfriend Valerie. I sat on a stool in front of my father, my arm outstretched and my finger pointing. My arm got tired. I realized, after what seemed like hours of photographs, that being a model was hard work. My fa-

My father in Idaho, 1961. © Virginia Aste

ther, Nickie, and the photographer, Edmund Shea, stayed very upbeat when I began to droop.

A professor of mine sent me a black-and-white photo of an enlargement of that picture. She had been in Mississippi on sabbatical and gone to the Seymour Lawrence Reading Room, seen this picture of me, and taken a quick snap of it.

I put the photo on the wall in my office. At first the picture upset me because I realized how much of myself I had forgotten. This little girl has a firm look on her face. She is unflinching. I had a nightmare about her. In the nightmare she walked

My mother and me in San Francisco, 1967.

towards me slowly to take my hand. I shook in terror as she advanced closer. I woke up, my heart beating fast in the dark, knowing that I had to stretch out my hand to her.

The End

Many biographers will make up endings for my father. I have run the end over and over and over in my mind. Since I know I can't change him, I change myself. Now that I'm older it would be different. I can pull him from the dark waters of Bolinas. A. Alvarez, in his book *The Savage God: A Study of Suicide,* says that suicide is like divorce and that people who attempt suicide are trying to get a kind of divorce from life. What Alvarez says that he realizes after surviving his own suicide attempt is that he could start his life again, the way one might start a new relationship.

His book helped me to understand a little bit of what my father's thought process might have been during this acute phase. My father had money problems, family problems, and drinking problems, but his biggest problem was that he didn't want to live.

The Last Word

*Soon the tomb would be complete and the door would be opened when
it was needed and someone would go inside to stay there for the ages.*

—R.B., *In Watermelon Sugar*

I've bought a plot for my dad in a small cemetery near a sea-
side town on the rocky northern California coast. An elderly
man, the volunteer caretaker, helped me with the purchase. There
is a sheep pasture on one side of the cemetery and a grove of
eucalyptus trees at the far end. The plot I purchased is at the top
near the shade of several creaking trees. My dad spent so much
time avoiding the sun I can't see putting him in direct afternoon
rays with no respite.

The caretaker is in his seventies and is a sheep rancher. He
knows the history of the cemetery and the church as well. Nor-
wegian shipbuilders built the immaculate white church which
sits down in the town. The church is so well built that if you
wanted to you could take the church down to the water, flip it
over, and float it down the coast to San Francisco.

I bought the plot a long, long time ago. I know the caretaker
is wondering why I haven't put a stone there yet, or better still,
why I haven't placed my father there. I know my father should
have a marker and a place. But placing a headstone would re-

quire knowing what I want carved in the stone. His ashes are sitting in a Japanese urn.

My stomach, the most honest gauge in this whole process, still churns when I think about burying him, so I don't. I have decided on white marble, and I have decided that I don't take having the last word lightly.

School

"I had the worst nightmare last night," my father said to me when I was fifteen.

"About what?" I asked, imagining vampires, witches, and car crashes, which were the familiar fare of my nightmares.

"School. I was back in school," he said with a worried look.

Deciding to get a B.A. felt like betrayal to me. Because of my upbringing, I never have become a true believer in academia, but I did love to learn. My married name protected me from the questions I fielded growing up. "Are you . . . ?" "What's it like being the daughter of . . . ?" Or the dreaded "Do you know who this is. . . ?"

When I graduated, it was important that all my names be on the diploma, because everyone had been there with me. At my graduation, I could see him sitting in the shade on a grassy knoll, an imposing figure as always, watching me as I reached out to take my diploma.

I didn't know my father had graduated from high school until he died and I found his diploma. Richard Gary Brautigan.

He had tucked a recent photo of himself in a triangle of purple ribbon that decorated each corner of the diploma. I think he meant for me to find it and make of it what I might.

My father came to visit me in a dream the month after I began to study for an advanced degree. We were sitting side by side in a lecture hall listening to a professor lecture on the symbolism of mothers. My father began to tell me something about his mother but was interrupted by a man sitting behind us. I stood up.

"Stop it! Let him finish," I said.

My father rose to his feet. But when he spoke his words were garbled, so he gave up talking and reached out and hugged me. Afterwards I was left standing alone in Golden Gate Park, looking at the gray fog, wondering how I had gotten so far from home.

Rehab

If I had my way I would put my father and Kurt Cobain in the same room.

"Daddy, this is Kurt Cobain. He is a young poet and a heroin addict. Kurt, this is my father, an old poet and alcoholic."

I would give them cups of coffee and inform them that they both have blue eyes, blond hair, and sad childhoods and were born in Tacoma, Washington.

After this brief introduction, large burly fellows would cart them off to the rehab home for brilliant young poets who fear they have nothing more left to say and brilliant old, broken poets whom no one wants to hear from anymore. My father would teach Kurt how to fly-fish, and Kurt might teach my father a few licks on the guitar.

"No. Easy. Float it. You're not going to catch any fish if you cast that chickenshit way."

"That sounds like fucking garbage. You have to turn the volume up and rip harder on that string."

What if when you go to heaven you are stationed according

to where you were born and the two of them are eating rainbow trout dipped in cornmeal fried in a cast-iron pan over a hot fire on a cool morning and after they wash up, they play haunting duets on electric guitars? The music they write together heals people as it drifts down past the stars towards a spinning white-and-blue, brown-and-green earth.

Tears from the Clouds

Two years after my father died, it stopped raining. A few storms came through, but nothing like the old days. My husband and I bought a house in Santa Rosa with a leaky roof and it didn't matter. Ten years after his death, it's raining again.

Sharing a doorway during a downpour with a man with a shopping cart full of aluminum cans: "An ark is in order, don't you think?"

"Yep." I smile.

I started writing about my father and me last summer. I laughed a lot remembering him. This winter I have cried remembering him, and he has wept with me. I fill tissues and my hands with tears. He fills whole storm fronts, crying down on my house for sometimes twenty-seven days at a time. Our ninety-two-year-old roof has given up and lets in the salty water. I put out pans to catch my father's tears. Once, the sound of his weeping was so loud, I woke my husband and we went out to the living room and stood in our underwear and watched the torrential midnight rain, reflected in the streetlight, enclose us in a watery blanket.

I sit and rock.

These tears don't hurt.

The rain keeps falling.

My father and I have needed to do this for a long time.

Blue Skies

Last night after a long absence, I dreamed about him. He read me a poem and added a stanza in the form of a question. I can see the perfectly placed lines on the page and his delicate fingers holding the edges of the paper: "I've written my life. What are we going to write about?" It was clear to me in the dream that he didn't mean him and that his message wasn't for me alone, he was referring to a whole new generation of writers.

When I awoke from the dream, I was smiling. And after far too much rain, the sky was blue.

"This day is beautiful," my daughter said to me as she ate her breakfast cereal.

Hands

My father was not bound by the rules of physicality that govern most men and women. He never felt obligated to rush forward and lift a heavy item. His hands were always smooth and white and were fascinating to watch. They gave a hint to his depth, flickering, almost luminous at times because he was so pale. Most of his hand movements were complex and beautiful. At times if he was perplexed or troubled his head would tilt and his arms would fly out and his hands would express this sadness. A great deal of the time they rested lightly on his hips and when he walked they led the way. And just this minute it occurred to me that the only time his hands were silenced was when he was drunk.

When he was thinking his hands would weave in and out of his hair. My daughter does this sometimes and it is startling.

Fears in the Night

My father was nervous about a lot of things. His fingernails were bitten down to the quick, and he was always absently nibbling at the little hangnail strings. At night before he went to bed, he checked the knobs on the gas stove to make sure they were off. Putting his hand out, he felt every black knob as though he didn't trust his eyes. And then, as if he didn't trust his hands, he came back again and again to look at the knobs until he was satisfied they were off. He did this with locked doors too, locking the door, pulling at the knob to make sure it was secure, starting out to the bus or road or down the hallway, and then going back and jiggling the doorknob one last time.

When I first got married I would lie in bed beside my husband, staring at the shadows on the wall and then asking him if the stove was off. A reasonable silence would be followed by "Why wouldn't the stove be off?"

"It could be on," I would say, imagining the black knob turned slightly to the left, letting hissing gas escape, permeating the house and ensuring our deaths.

His Icelandic great-grandmother believed in elves and left a piece of cloth in the door when she left the farm, which wasn't often, so she would know if the elves had come.

"Humph." *Thud, thud, thud,* followed by a soft sigh as he slid back in bed.

"Off."

Only the half-buried memory of his great-grandmother made it possible for my husband to make that trip to the kitchen in the dark to check what he knew was off. But elves are small and have only limited power over tired husbands. The silence got longer and longer with each of my requests until one night he fell asleep without answering. I stopped asking and tiptoed into the kitchen to check the stove myself. The knobs were always tightly off.

Visits

My father's ghost visits me often. He comes at unexpected times, mostly to help me out of a tight spot. In the beginning I was afraid of his ghost. The nights right after his body was found, I asked my father-in-law, who is a doctor, for sleeping pills. Wisely, he did not give them to me. He let me find out on my own that fears of my father appearing to me mangled and decomposed were not real. When my father did appear, he was whole, and I was trying to catch up with his long-legged gait.

He turned his head and said, not unkindly, "I've got to go. I have a lot of things to do."

I woke up alone in the dim light of an empty fall morning, staring at the ceiling.

He came to see my daughter when she was born. He didn't say anything. He just reached out one of his long fingers to touch her little one. And when Elizabeth was five, she told me that Grandpa had come to visit her in her dream.

"What did you do?" I said, trying not to sound alarmed.

"Played," she said indignantly, as if the idea of any other activity was ridiculous.

"I sat on his lap and he gave me some candy and then we played."

Most of his visits are not profound. He comes, instead, to remind me that life is not so serious.

As I tagged along with Cadence, who was doing business in Aspen, staying at five-star hotels with the very rich, I began to get overly concerned about my clothes. Maybe *this* would look more acceptable, I thought to myself, as I held up an outfit to the mirror in the dressing area.

My father walked into the suite at the Little Nell, eating a red plum, his hair wispy, arms bare, wearing a T-shirt.

"Ianthe, who are you trying to kid? Stop chickenshitting around about your clothes."

"But these people wear watches that cost more than my house," I protested.

A shrug of his shoulders was his reply.-

I put on my jeans, a clean white T-shirt, and my battered Timex watch and went down to the lobby.

My father in San Francisco, 1972. © Ianthe Brautigan Swensen

Three Dreams

Explanations

In my dream last night, my father killed himself again. Cadence sat on a kitchen chair in his apartment while I searched through his papers for a suicide note. Box after box of papers turned up no trace. I woke up crying. I still don't know what to make of the dream. Does it mean that I have finally convinced my subconscious that he is dead? If so, will I never dream of him again? Or does it mean that something new is about to occur?

Elizabeth and her best friend are taking turns typing ghost stories on her Royal typewriter. The same Royal my dad gave me twenty-five years ago. I walk in and her friend is typing and Elizabeth is reading. When I return, Elizabeth is typing and her friend is reading. I don't ask them what they are doing, and they don't offer any explanations.

He's Not Dead, Again

Just after I dreamed he committed suicide and was dead, I dreamed with just as much clarity that my father was alive. I was overjoyed. I went around telling everyone in the dream that he was alive. He and I sat down together in a huge wood-framed house, and I gave him his life back, piece by piece, paper by paper. The relief I felt in doing so was enormous. When I woke up, I almost burst out laughing.

The Porch Dream

I dream about a refrigerator with open doors and an electrical short in the box. The blue sparks draw me towards it. The interior is white and empty except for two brown textured heads. They look like African masks. Their eyes are hollow and black, holding an expression of suffering. I gently push past them and end up in my father's kitchen in Montana. It is late at night. The kitchen is empty and all the lights are on. I walk out the back door onto his porch and stand there holding a paper bag that contains everything I own. I can see the little tree I tied my horse to and a white cast-iron bathtub that was always there for no particular reason that I knew of. The barn still presides over everything. The night air is clean against my skin, but I know that the crumpled grocery bag I am holding doesn't contain enough to change anything.

Christmas

After my stepmother left him, my father and I had a conversation in the large living room of his Green Street apartment in San Francisco in 1979. The rug was gone, the stereo was gone. Only the couches and a strange octagonal table remained. We sat together in the cavernous living room, the only light coming from the hallway and the fireplace because the lamps were gone as well. He gave me a check for $150. We were just sitting when he put his glass of whiskey down and jumped up.

"I'll be right back."

I laid my right hand on the cold imitation leather, holding the check with my other. His signature was thin and intricate and fixed in its uniqueness.

After a few moments he returned, holding a file folder. He carefully extracted a picture from it.

"This is your grandmother," he said.

I paused before looking at the picture. I wondered where he had gotten a picture of a woman he had not seen in twenty-five years. My father stood across the room from me. Then I studied the Polaroid of a middle-aged woman with brown hair sitting on a stone bench under a weeping willow tree next to an Asian-looking man. The man looked peaceful. His pants were rolled up and he wore a white undershirt. My grandmother was dressed in Capri pants, her legs crossed, leaning forward holding a cigarette. Her eyes were alive, burning a hole through time. After a minute or so, my father leaned forward.

"Are you done looking?"

"Yes," I said.

"Are you sure?"

I nodded my head.

He walked over to the fireplace, took the picture with his long delicate fingers, and held it on the flames.

We watched together as the picture tumbled and caught fire. He turned and looked at me.

"The last time I saw my mother I had just been released from the mental hospital in Salem."

I held my breath.

He continued talking. "I was committed after I threw rocks at the police station window, hoping that they would arrest me and give me a meal. I was hungry. Instead, they put me in a mental institution."

He reached down, picked up his drink.

"I realized that I had made a big fucking mistake." He paused for a moment, and then his voice became very matter-of-fact. "So I did my best to get out of there as fast as I could. I became a model patient." My heart was beating fast.

"How long did it take you to get out?"

"Three months."

"Did they give you shock treatments?"

"Yes."

Suddenly, his overcautiousness with electricity made sense. As a small child, I found it amazing that my father was afraid of changing lightbulbs.

My father walked over to the window and turned his back on me. I wanted to call out to him to open the window. I thought maybe if the foggy San Francisco air were allowed to flow into the room it could calm my stomach and would somehow heal my father.

Now, looking back, I think he was considering suicide, again, and wanted to make sure that I knew everything there was to know about his past before he died. He didn't want me to find out from a newspaper or a magazine.

We never talked about his mother or his hospital stay again. That night became a ten-year-old shadowy conversation. Sometimes I'm tempted to take a sponge and some soap and wash away all the shadowy conversations, but they are all I have left.

Mary Lou

After thirty-two years of silence, my Aunt Barbara has sent me pictures of my relatives and my father as a child. My Aunt Barbara has a clear way of speaking that reminds me of my father. She loved my father dearly. He raised her, she told me. It was his job to baby-sit her while their mother worked. "Richard never seemed to mind, but we did spend a lot of time fishing," she laughed. My Aunt Barbara has a wonderful laugh. When my father hunted out of season he made Barbara carry the pheasants he shot under her coat. He figured that the game warden wouldn't search a little girl. "Richard was so good to me that I would do anything for him, even carry a dead bird under my jacket," she said.

"We would make peanut butter sandwiches and quart jars of Kool-Aid and walk for miles fishing along the way. He saw beauty in everything," she said. "We were just kids, but he would point out a special tree or the way the flowers were bending in the wind. Nobody talked about that sort of thing in our family or even in the town we lived."

The photographs are stunning. My great-grandmother Bessie

My great-grandmother Bessie, around 1930. Permission of Barbara Fitzhugh

is dressed in an elegant silk dress with jet dangling earrings. I resemble my father's legendary Uncle Edward, whom my father wrote about in the poem "1942." I decided to break the decades-old silence imposed by my father about his mother. My Aunt Barbara gave me her name and her phone number and this admonition: "She's not an easy woman."

One day I called my grandmother Mary Lou on the phone. Much to my surprise, she answered.

"Hello."

With my heart pounding, I spoke quickly. I was terrified that she would hang up on me. "This is Richard's daughter, Ianthe."

A long silence.

I didn't let her speak. I told her what I wanted. My history.

*My great-uncle Edward
around 1940.*
Permission of
Barbara Fitzhugh

"I have to turn the stove off and get a cup of tea."

"I'll wait," I said.

"Don't go," she said. "Don't go."

"I won't."

I listened to her sigh in pain as she sat down in a chair. "I have compression fractures in my back."

"Are you seeing a doctor?"

"He's not any good. All the good doctors are dead."

"How old are you?"

"Eighty-five. No one in our family has lived this long."

"Do you want to live to be ninety?"

"Oh, heavens, no. But I might miss something if I don't. How much do you weigh?"

"One hundred and forty-seven pounds."

"Why, you big fat slob."

I started laughing, "Mary Lou, I'm almost six feet tall. You must be tiny."

"I am."

· · ·

A black hole of nothingness became a cacophony of names and dates. She told me about my great-grandmother Bessie, who really was a bootlegger. Bessie made and sold moonshine whiskey during Prohibition and then worked as a cook in Tacoma, Washington.

After moving out of the family home, Mary Lou and my father lived above a candy factory in Tacoma and she waitressed. She didn't have a refrigerator. "Back then, you bought your food one day at a time." She didn't want to talk about Bernard Brautigan. "I left him with everything I owned in a paper sack. I didn't even know that I was pregnant." But she did tell me that her grandparents had run a poorhouse in Missouri.

"Do you know what a poorhouse is?"

"No."

"It's a place were people go to live who have no money."

Mary Lou loved to rattle off dates. My newly found relatives were living and dying at such a fast rate I could barely hold on to them, but I was afraid to ask her to slow down.

"You have such a good memory," I told her.

"Did you know your father had a photostatic memory?"

I knew that she meant photographic. "Yes."

"Did you know that he was six foot six inches tall when he was twenty-one years old? He was an excellent shot at a moving target with his left hand. Not many right-handers shoot with their left hand, you know."

I realized she was getting tired.

Finally she said off handedly, "I'm tired of carrying all this around."

I asked if I could call her again.

"All right. We don't know each other very well, do we?"

"No. Good-bye, Mary Lou."

"Good-bye . . . love," she said.

Shock Therapy

I met a woman with a limp when I was nine years old. I asked her what happened. She told me that she was from the South and that when she was sixteen years old she and a friend had been wild, so the parents got together and decided to have the girls treated with electric shock therapy. A strap broke during her procedure and she was left with a limp. Her friend calmed down so much that all she wanted to do was put hand cream on her hands.

Once I was listening to a talk show and a soft-spoken caller was saying she had been told that if she wanted to get out of the state facility she had been in she needed to submit to the treatments. "I lost big chunks of my memory," she said.

My father told me lots of stories from his childhood. He worked in a pickle factory after he left high school. "I rode in with the loads of cucumbers and ate tiny gherkins out of a pickling barrel in the factory until that last fateful bite. Overload!" he said with a laugh. "I didn't eat another gherkin for years." He told me this story while happily munching on a gherkin.

That night I kept adjusting the dial on my radio, hoping to

hear better what the soft-spoken woman was saying. But after a while I gave up. Her voice was too faint.

They sentenced my young, idealistic, very innocent father, whose only mistake was trying to make a living as a writer in the small town of Eugene, Oregon, in 1955, to the Salem State Mental Hospital. Once there, they gave him much-needed regular meals, and shock treatments, and nightmares for the rest of his life. Back in the early fifties, they didn't use any anesthesia with this procedure. They strapped my father down, put a rubber bit in his teeth so he wouldn't bite his tongue off, and turned on the current.

In the dark silence I realized that I'll never know whether my father lost memory in all that electrical current. The woman lost about two weeks of her life. She said that she didn't think she had "missed anything important."

Recently I called my father-in-law.

"What did they call the treatments?"

"EST," he replied.

"Did you ever see any patients after they had it done?"

"Oh, sure," he said, "but the last ones were back in the seventies. I didn't think they did it anymore."

"Did the patients you saw lose memory afterward?"

"Sometimes. But most remembered everything about what happened and how painful the treatment was. They also used insulin shock therapy back then. They would inject patients with enough insulin to throw them into an insulin shock. That was all they had. They didn't have any of the drugs they have today."

I told him the story the woman had told me about her experience in the South.

He was doubtful. "They only used EST on schizophrenics or manic depressives."

"What about my dad?" I hesitated for a moment. What I

wanted to ask was if he thought that my dad was crazy. "What do you think EST did for him?"

"EST didn't work most of the time, and when it did, you had to get the treatments again."

"So, since my dad was relatively sane for the rest of his life, he probably wasn't mentally ill?"

"Probably."

This logic gives me a sense of relief. My father could have been profoundly depressed. And I do know that they still use EST to treat cases of depression that don't respond to anything else. Some people, like the woman I heard on the radio, say EST has been their salvation. But my father never said he was glad they shocked him week after week. "A kind of mini–electric chair," my father-in-law called it.

Some years later my father wrote a poem entitled:

INSANE ASYLUM

PART 8

*Baudelaire went
to the insane asylum
disguised as a
psychiatrist.
He stayed there
for two months
and when he left,
the insane asylum
loved him so much
that it followed
him all over
California,
and Baudelaire
laughed when the
insane asylum
rubbed itself
up against his
leg like a
strange cat.*

Quest

I decided to visit the Pacific Northwest, to fulfill a lifetime wish to see where my father came from and what he fled. I could swear I heard my father laughing. He was egging me on, as only he could. "Go. It's a quest. It's a goddamn medieval pilgrimage to honor your long-suffering dead father." I'm going to walk the same paths he did, look at the same trout streams he did, see the house he lived in.

All this despite the fact that I'm not sure I'm strong enough to tolerate his pain that originates from there. My fantasy is that I will recognize the magic as well. But this seems unwise, because if the magic were that strong he would still be alive.

My father in Idaho, 1961. © Virginia Aste

"The Past Is Not Dead. It's Not Even Past."—William Faulkner

I went to Oregon in a dream. I was shown the house my father grew up in. The front door had small lead-crystal windows that sparkled in the sun. The fields nearby were bathed in a golden light. My grandmother was huddled in the corner of an old chicken coop, crying. I could see my father lying dead on an old dirt road. I walked slowly up to him and knelt down beside his body to look at him more closely. His blue eyes flew open. Cadence appeared and grabbed my arm, and we ran and ran and ran.

The Wind

Cadence likes to drive fast. She likes to feel the back end of her car unhook from the road. When her boyfriend has had enough, he doesn't say "Slow down!" Instead he yells, "I'm afraid! I'm afraid!"

An east wind has been blowing for three days, bringing dappled light throughout the house, along with lots of pollen and fear. The woman at the orthodontist's office doesn't notice how fearful I am. My husband, Paul, sits on the back porch and reassures me. His deep tenor voice isn't shaken by the wind. "You can live," he says over and over again. We aren't talking about death even. And the words he speaks aren't actually the ones I quoted. His real words are: You can go to the Pacific Northwest. Be careful, but everything will be all right.

The wind keeps blowing, stirring up clouds of uncertainty in me. I need hot summer days to warm my bones and still my thoughts. I see death when I look into this wind. I worry about losing everyone. No one seems safe. I fear for Paul's health. I think about all the danger that Elizabeth is exposed to every day. She wants to walk to school. She wants to ride her bike to school. Occasionally, she wants to be an astronaut. One day in the car she says, "Remember when I was in preschool and wanted to be an astronaut?" I nod my head.

"I would have a vision."

I looked at her curiously. "A vision?"

She clarifies. "A dream that happens when you are awake, except you think it."

"What was your vision?"

"I would take a spaceship up in the clouds and bring back a piece of cloud in a glass box for you to see."

"That's a beautiful idea."

"But I'm not going to be an astronaut now."

"What are you going to be?"

"You know."

"I just want to hear you say it."

"A snake doctor."

My husband and I take turns taking her to a monthly herpetology meeting. Everyone brings their iguana or snake and sits in folding chairs, listening to different speakers. It's easy to spot those people who have iguanas; they all have deep scratches on their arms. Sometimes it's boring and Elizabeth falls asleep on my husband's shoulder. She won't leave early because of the raffle they hold at the end of the meeting.

Elizabeth is smart and careful, yet I want to go to school with her and watch over her unseen, making sure no harm comes her way. Luckily, the principal frowns on parents loitering in the hallways. He is a good man who watches over his school. On Halloween, he dressed like a shepherd complete with a large crook. Elizabeth dressed as a snake charmer.

I worry because I see my father's fear and despair in me. I

wonder if I'm infected with his suicide. I feel like a door has been left unlocked, a dangerous exit. Can I handle any more death or tragedy? Is there a limit to how much horror one can tolerate? What is the effect of suffering on the soul? Will it shape my feet like an odd-fitting pair of shoes? And the problem is that there are so many potential deaths in the future. Despite these thoughts, I drink my coffee and I feed the orphan, an orange Manx cat, that has taken up residence under the boat in our driveway.

My husband and Elizabeth think we should adopt the cat. I remind him the animal hair is overwhelming already. "He could be an outside cat," he replies.

"And the snake doesn't have hair," Elizabeth reminds me. I pretend to be fearless and make my daughter breakfast, get her lunch money, and remind her to take a sweater because the wind is blowing. I write, almost surprised that the words aren't blown off the page.

I'm finding that Cadence's love of the blacktop is contagious. Later that night on the way home from San Francisco State, I decide to get in the fast lane and enjoy the feel of the turns in the road on the descent from the rainbow tunnel. I go sixty miles an hour and feel like I'm going a hundred because I can see other people's brake lights around me. They don't know this road as well as I do. So, for a while, I pretend I'm a daredevil riding a motorcycle.

Cutting

Each step I took on my journey seemed wrong. The wind kept blowing. My father said that you feel off when the wind blows because of the negative ions. Thunder and lightning swept through Santa Rosa last week, which was very unusual for the month of June. Montana came to visit me. I have been trying to write, but the conflict police had set up camp in my small, cramped office. They stalked me, filling the room with cigarette smoke.

"What are you doing?"

"What are you writing?"

The dog slept oblivious in the living room.

I found solace outside trimming bushes and pulling weeds. I felt subversive escaping from under the glare of all the condemnation that I had created within myself. I was drowning in the voices that indicted me.

I should have saved him.

Standing with the electric trimmer in hand, I balanced on the fence trying to reach the top of a tall bush. My neighbor saw me and yelled, "Don't cut your foot off." I couldn't very well tell him that a small, neat gash had crossed my mind. But I cut leaves instead. They fell in a cool shower across my shoulders.

When I was finished, I was in one piece, all my fingers and toes. I was wearied by the impulse to cause myself pain. I stood still until it passed.

I had been running from my computer for the last three weeks. I had sanded, painted, cleaned, and worried.

"When are you going to write?" my husband asked me.

This morning before he left the house, he told Elizabeth to tell me to write. I asked her to get dressed and she pointed at me fiercely and said in her most stern voice, "Write!" Since she looks so much like me, there was an interesting moment of connection.

"Okay, okay," I laughed.

And three hours later, here I was, facing a paralyzing fear. Bringing my father into my house was a dangerous thing to do, because then I had the complex task of keeping him whole.

I grew up knowing my father's fear. I stood by watching it materialize and grip him. My earliest memory of this was seeing a certain look in his eyes along with the hesitation in the way he moved his body. He would look down the street, not seeing the apartment buildings or the wind blowing the trees on Bay Street in San Francisco. Standing beside him, watching this transformation, I knew he was scared. At four years old, I looked up and down the street, but I couldn't see anything that he should be afraid of.

My father began suffering from severe insomnia when I was about seven or eight. When I came to visit, he greeted me with a report on how many hours he had slept. A good night was six or seven and a bad night was four or five. At those moments standing there in the hallway of the Geary Street apartment, looking up at him, I knew I needed to help him, and I invented a hundred different ways. I knew the right questions to ask. I got good at asking questions that intrigued him into long answers that could keep him alive for years at a time.

At fourteen, listening to his explanations of why he shot holes in the wall or axed the kitchen ceiling or how I prevented him from killing himself, there was never a time for me to be afraid. I never cried. I couldn't even breathe. These were not times to be afraid. Whenever the fear rose within my father, I became as still as possible and faced the crashing wall of helplessness that was coming down around us both.

Cadence was going with me to the McKenzie River in Oregon in August. My stomach tightened every time I thought about the trip. I would have to try to see my grandmother, even if she kicked me out. I wanted to stand on the sidewalk and look at the house where my father spent his teenage years. I wanted to stand on the banks of the rivers and streams that my father fished in. I would probably get poison oak, as my father did. I wanted to see what killed him.

Another Suicide

Don Carpenter, a fine novelist, was one of my father's best friends. One night Don Carpenter's daughter called. She told me that her father had committed suicide. She hadn't wanted me to find out from the newspaper. I didn't cry right away. I made dinner; I mowed the lawn; I folded the laundry.

After my father's death, Don called me to give me advice. His friends called him the Telephone Buddha. I don't drink because of Don and a short conversation we had about the subject. Instead of saying, "I hope you're not drinking to avoid the grief and do you realize alcoholism runs in your family," he asked, "Do you drink?"

"Rarely. Maybe a couple of glasses of wine a month," I said.

"Why?" he said. Then, "Do you know that your father helped me to stop drinking?"

"How?" I asked incredulously, knowing my father and how much he drank.

"I had stopped eating and had just been drinking for days, and I called your father up drunk and incoherent. He told me to get a piece of paper because I wasn't going to remember the conversation. Richard told me to write the word EAT. When I woke up I read the note and went and got something to eat. It was the first meal I had had in a week. Remembering to eat kept me alive long enough to figure some things out, like that I needed to stop drinking."

His "Why?" echoed for several days after this conversation until I stopped drinking. Whenever I think about having a glass of wine, I don't because I can still hear his dry, sardonic voice.

As I jaywalked across the sunny, well-to-do Mill Valley street on the way to a memorial service being held for Don Carpenter at the Book Depot, I tried to bargain with myself about his right to commit suicide. He had been battling serious health issues for years. People do kill themselves for reasons that have nothing to do with depression or despair. They don't want to suffer through long terrible illnesses, and in some cultures suicide is acceptable for other reasons as well. I tried to accept the way he chose to die, ignoring the nausea that had begun to build. Michael McClure mentioned that Don was one of the few people who had managed to hold on to his friendship with my father until his death. I cried. In Don's obituary in *The New York Times* I read that Don never got over my father's suicide and that was why he, too, committed suicide. I almost threw up reading that explanation.

I remembered a man named Harlow, who had died of cancer a few weeks earlier than Don. He had decided to die the long, hideous way, literally touching the people around him until he stopped breathing. He held his young children, reassured his wife, and joked around with his friends. What about Harlow's choice?

Two days later, I slowly drifted into a profound depression, a kind of doubling of my father's suicide. Luckily, Elizabeth was at camp. Every morning I awoke preparing and expecting to spend the day alone but somebody showed up at my door. My friends who liked to shop took me shopping with them. My friends who liked to organize came over to my house and helped me put things away. My sister Ellen called me on the phone and told me it was all right. Cadence railed, as only she can, at suicide. I didn't have anything to say at all. Once again, it was all my fault my father died. Thus it was all my fault Don killed himself as well.

Somehow I managed to get Elizabeth packed for the trip to Oregon. I bought her books to read, rented twenty hours of books on tape to make the trip a bit more bearable, and packed food. I found the sleeping bags for Cadence and myself, got the car serviced, and tried to remember what I was supposed to take. Money. My grandmother's address, which I found on a postcard dated 1956, from one of my father's rejection notices. Sunglasses. Chap Stick. Journal. Camera. Candy. Maps. Lots and lots of maps.

Road Trip

There were so many blackberries back in there that it was hard to believe. They were huge like black diamonds but it took a lot of medieval blackberry engineering, chopping entrances and laying bridges, to be successful like the siege of a castle.

"The castle has fallen!"

Sometimes when I got bored with picking blackberries I used to look into the deep shadowy dungeon-like places way down in the vines. You could see things that you couldn't make out down there and shapes that seemed to change like phantoms.

—R.B., "Blackberry Motorist,"
in *Revenge of the Lawn*

Part 1: What you lose and what is returned to you

What you find is rarely what you think will be there. As a child I used to hope and dream about the places my parents were going to take me. What they found beautiful was always puzzling to me. My father pointed everything out to me as though it would disappear if I didn't see what he saw. A pattern of clouds, the angle of a tree, a small bird sitting on a rusting string of barbed wire. I do this for my daughter also. It is good training for a writer or a budding scientist. I remembered this as Cadence, Elizabeth, and I traveled through the middle of California on Highway 5 up past the Oregon border through the glistening river town of Klamath Falls in the white Volvo, or the Vulvena, as Cadence has christened it. After making fun of my car for a couple of years, it turned out that she liked driving the Volvo. "It can turn on a dime!"

I looked out the window longingly at Klamath Falls as we drove by but there was no time to stop. I will come back another time, I promised myself.

The plan was that Elizabeth would stay in Bend while Cadence and I went over the mountains to Eugene to visit my grandmother. Bend was immaculate compared to the Bay Area. In Bend, they pumped your gas and there was no litter or homelessness, and there was a great deal of new construction. "This town gives me the creeps," Cadence said. "Where is the decay?" Elizabeth and her best friend had a joyful reunion, and after ten hours of driving we were happy to be closer to our ultimate destination.

Before we left Bend, we bought bug spray. Cadence drove. I sat surrounded by maps, which had long since lost their crisp, creased qualities and now had become wrinkled and confusing because I could never quite figure out how to refold them. One of the maps we needed had a big black marking-pen line drawn by one of Cadence's boyfriend's former girlfriends. The fat black line obscured vital information.

"Why would someone mark a map this way? It's nearly impossible to ever use it again."

Cadence nodded. "Well, that was one of the reasons she is now an ex-girlfriend." I was glad because I liked Charlie.

After we left Bend we headed toward the Cascade Range, which we needed to cross to reach Eugene. After miles of nothing but pine trees we suddenly came across black lava beds. The road was literally cut through the center of a blanket of dark metamorphic rock. Once we reached the top there was a small parking lot filled with tourists. They were all ascending and descending a black tower made of lava rock. After a couple of hours of being alone on the road it was a shock to see people, all of whom seemed to have no cares. They were on vacation. Some had brought their pets with them. We had to stop on the sharp, jagged stairs for small dogs who were being urged by their masters to hop up just one more step. Cadence rolled her eyes. The top was not really worth it even though we were told that if we looked out each of the windows we could see a different mountain. The range called the Three Sisters was there, off in the distance. We both shivered in the cold wind.

We decided to avoid the main highway and instead came down the other side the mountain on a stretch of old highway that was so narrow and curvy that RVs were prohibited. In what seemed like minutes but was actually an hour or so, the landscape became dramatically different. The predominating color was no longer black but green. Scotts Lake, Adler Springs, Indian Ford, Frog Creek, White Branch Creek, Proxy Creek; each road sign we passed, I tried to absorb the name along with the growing awareness of how beautiful was the place where my father spent most of his childhood. Delicate ferns were tucked in the roots of trees that the winter storms had exposed. A canopy of branches was filtering the sunlight into lacelike patterns on the dashboard and Cadence's hands as she held the steering wheel. The greenness absorbed everything; even the car engine was muted. This was one of the rare times in my life that my expectation of the destination was surpassed.

I knew that my father had to have tried the fishing wherever there was water. As a boy he had spent the same type of exacting artistry in fishing all the different waterways around the McKenzie River that he had as an adult writing books.

I unrolled the car window and listened for water. There were

My father trout fishing in Idaho, 1961. © Virginia Aste

no other cars on the road. For an hour we were suspended above the river. Wildflowers clung to the hillside. Around every blind curve, I thought I could hear water. As the road leveled out and we reached the bottom, I knew that this meant we were near the river. My heart started beating faster. I had thought everything was going to be gloomy and overcast. Instead the sun was shining down on us like a generous heart. I was scared. I was going to have to get out of the car. "Do you think it's this sunny all the time?" I asked Cadence. She had lived up near Woodland, Washington, for a couple of years when she was a kid.

"No," she said. "If it's anything like Washington there are times when all it does is rain." When I looked at Cadence she wasn't frightened; she was excited about making camp. She hated hotels and had almost convinced me that I would rather be camping.

The perfect campground appeared, Limberlost. Cadence placed her wallet on top of the Volvo and when we excitedly drove off to unpack our stuff at the perfect campsite, her wallet flew off the top of the car. After pitching our tent by the creek, Cadence realized it was gone. We searched everywhere, including the ranger station to check the lost and found. After mourning the loss of all Cadence's identification and credit cards, we went and had a greasy lunch at a nearby lodge. For a moment or two, while waiting for our food, we both got a little tense thinking that this trip needed to be looked after. But then we realized the odds of us both losing our wallets was small and more important that there wasn't any structure to this odd quest, except to visit my grandmother. I ate blackberries from the bushes down behind the lodge on the river. There were huge blackberries everywhere, and I could see the ripples on the water through the bushes.

When we got back to the campground, we went for a hike and climbed a steep hillside of moss-covered boulders. The moss was dried because the summer had been unseasonally warm. I began to annoy Cadence by asking her if she thought there might be snakes in these rocks. We split up after that, Cadence to sketch and I to hike up the narrow creek, all the while scanning the bushes for poison oak. Teaching me what poison oak looks like was one of the first of many survival skills my father taught me.

The creek was crystal clear with the foliage creating almost perfect rooms everywhere. The sky was becoming slightly over-cast, but it was still warm. I looked for places that my father might have fished. The sound of the rushing water was sooth-ing. A part of my father was everywhere pulling back the foliage with his long slender fingers, reading each molecule of water with his blue eyes. I sat on a gray fallen log, ferns growing out of its knotholes, and watched the water slide over the rocks. Suddenly I became terribly homesick. I missed my daughter and my husband and the dog. I wanted to go home. I had seen enough. Enough. Enough. I lay back on the gray log and closed my eyes and listened to all the trout sneaking by me.

Back at the campsite we lit a fire and ate a freeze-dried meal. When the wood burned out, we decided to head back to the same lodge where we had had lunch to get a piece of blackberry pie and make phone calls. After each of us took a turn standing in the phone booth, which was lit by a blue fluorescent light in stark contrast to the dark woods, we were both very tired.

Once we got back to the campground, our neighbors gave us five perfect rainbow trout. Cadence had commented on how rude it was for them to have parked the bow of their boat in our campsite. They didn't move the boat, but they gave us fish, still icy cold from having just being cleaned in the stream. I held them, feeling a long-ago physical sensation, the smooth-slippery feel of trout. As a child I had fished with my father. And when I had gotten old enough to handle a knife, he had taught me how to clean them. These were already cleaned. I walked down to the creek in the dark and rinsed my hands. The fish were so fresh they didn't leave a smell.

"And just how are we going to cook these fish in the morn-ing?" Cadence asked. "We have no more firewood."

"We're having fish for breakfast," I said.

Cadence shrugged, and we crawled into the tent Cadence had borrowed from her boyfriend and fell asleep to the sound of running water.

In the morning Cadence tried to start a fire with the cardboard from the firewood box we had brought and some tree bark. Everyone in the campground had fished except for one couple two campsites away. They had a roaring fire and the man was in the middle of preparing what appeared at a distance to be a small feast: fried potatoes, bacon, but no fish. I walked over with my trout and traded some of the fish for some firewood, tinfoil, a pat of butter, and hot chocolate. The man turned out to be a chef. With giant tongs, he plucked a huge piece of burning wood from his fire and walked it over to our fire. He shook his head at the smoking bark and left us with enough wood to cook our fish. I made a little frying pan out of the tinfoil, melted the butter, and cooked the trout. I hadn't eaten freshly caught trout since my father died. The fish had a nice crisp skin and light flaky flesh.

For this part of the journey, I pulled out the map that my husband had found for me. Cadence and I then followed the McKenzie River trail down towards Eugene. I was constantly awake to the fact and kept repeating it as if it were a mantra. My dad was here. My dad was here. This was where he had hitchhiked as a boy. I hadn't expected the mystery to be so beautiful. In the middle of the hike to Sahalie Falls a bee stung me on the leg. I slowly became convinced that I was going to have an allergic reaction to the beesting and die out in the wilderness. I took notice; my fingers were swollen. I was hiking ahead of Cadence and wondered when I should break the news to her. Finally, after about five minutes, I cleared my throat.

· "Cadence, my hands are swollen."

"So are mine. It's the altitude." And then as if reading my mind she said, "You're going to be fine. You're not going to die out here." Her words were reassuring. I bathed my leg in the ice-cold water that roared across the rocks.

The descent toward Eugene began, I wanted to stop in Vida, a town after whom my father had named a character in *The Abortion.* I alternated between looking at the map, marking the distance to Vida, and glancing out the window of the car, watching the drift boats fishing.

There was a tiny roadside diner perched on the side of the road in the town of Vida. In reality it was a disguised single-wide trailer. Sunshine poured through the windows onto the immaculate floors. The small booths were filled with stern old people eating lunch and reading the Sunday paper. We sat at the counter.

Cadence and I ordered sandwiches and pie. While we waited for our food, I stared at all the people eating and wanted to ask them if they remembered a tall blond young man who might have stopped in twenty-five years ago on a day like this for a Coke and maybe a piece of pie. Nobody looked at me. The waitress couldn't have been more than sixteen years old. She ignored us as if it pained her to look at us because we belonged to a larger world. Two boys about eleven years old entered the store carrying fishing poles. They carefully leaned their fishing gear against the window and sat down at the counter kitty-corner from us. The boys spent a great deal of time counting their money and deciding what to order. One of them, intrigued by the sandwich Cadence had ordered, asked her what kind of sandwich it was.

"A club," she answered.

He nodded soberly and turned back to his friend and the continuing conversation about money and what to order. Neither the waitress nor the other customers even glanced at the boys. Finally the waitress took their carefully considered order without comment.

After I started eating my pie, I asked the boys how far they had walked to get to the diner. The boys became animated, turning on their stools and pointing in the direction that Cadence and I were headed. Three miles was the consensus, and then the one sitting closest to me added, "There isn't much to do up here."

"It sure is pretty, though," I said, and I went back to my lemon meringue pie, but now I felt their eyes on me and the camera that was sitting on the counter next to me.

"What are doing here?" one boy asked.

Cadence lifted her head from the newspaper she was reading. I thought she would like to know the answer to this question as well. The whole diner seemed to be listening at this point.

I said, "My dad used to fish up here when he was a teenager." And then I directed my attention to the waitress, who was looking out the window at the road and the cars that were driving past. "How long has this diner been here?"

She looked at me and shrugged her shoulders and then nodded her head to an older couple who were eating in a corner booth. "They would know."

The woman stopped eating and told me that the old diner had been here but had burned down.

"So, the old diner was right here where we are sitting, but this is just a new building?"

"Yes," and then she went back to eating.

"How long was the old diner here?"

"Forty-five years. Marie cooked back then."

I stretched and stood up to look at the pictures on the wall, which, I realized, were of the old diner before it burned down. I asked the boys if I could take a picture of their fishing poles leaning against the wall. They giggled and said sure. When I glanced at Cadence, I got the impression that she was ready to leave Vida. I told her I just wanted to take a picture of the town sign and take a look at the small creek nearby. I paid the bill and took the camera and walked briskly toward the town's sign. The creek was small, not promising as far as fish go, but I found more blackberry bushes. I stopped and began eating the largest, most juicy blackberries I'd ever had until my fingers were stained purple. I could see Cadence leaning against the car with her eyes closed, waiting.

"What were you doing?"

"Eating blackberries."

She looked as if she wanted to say something but had thought better of it.

We continued to follow the river towards Eugene. Everything became a blur of warm summer air; so many shades of green that I felt drugged. The river was never out of sight for more than a few minutes. Summer cabins lined the banks, because we were out of the national park, and then abruptly we were out of the mountains and driving through the small, almost flat valleys just before we reached Eugene.

The small two-lane highway we had been traveling on for so long became a freeway. I started fumbling with road maps and the AAA book for motels. The color changed to gray. Many thousands of cubic yards of cement had been poured to create the overpasses and the sidewalks and strip malls. The river disappeared. We narrowed our search for lodging down to an area close to the University of Oregon that had motels in our price range. The young, hip desk clerk with a modern haircut jolted us back to the present. Everyone we had met so far on this trip had been outdated by about twenty-five years as far as clothes and hairstyles. The clerk was a wealth of information. Her parents had attended the same schools that my father had. She circled where they were located on the map, and I looked forward to seeing his high school the next day.

We flipped on the TV. It was a relief to hear the sound of a cheesy seventies horror movie flood the room, *Tales from the Crypt*. While the little girl was letting the demented Santa in to kill her mother, Joan Collins, Cadence stared at one of my legs. "Did I burn your leg last night with that piece of wood?" She had knocked a piece of wood out of the fire pit and it had hit my leg.

Glancing down, I said, "Yes, I think you did."

Then Cadence shook her head. "That isn't a burn. It's a stupid blackberry stain."

She was right, just blackberries. I took my tennis shoes off and showed them to Cadence. The white soles were covered with blackberry stains. I put in yet another call to my grandmother and listened to the phone ring, almost relieved that she didn't answer. "So the plan for tomorrow?" Cadence asked.

"Go to my grandmother's and hope she lets me in."

Cadence wanted to get a present for her boyfriend. This and camping were the only requests she had made on this trip.

After a bad but expensive dinner, we went back to the hotel. I called to see how my daughter was and found out that she had gotten lost in the woods for about twenty minutes. Elizabeth told me that she and her friend had been playing a game involving following certain-shaped clouds, and they ended up lost. "We're not going to the woods, again," she said with a slightly shaky laugh.

I questioned once again the wisdom of traveling to Eugene. I had never gone on a quest before, looking for answers about the past. Most folks left well enough alone. Elizabeth's getting lost felt like a retaliation. "See what happens if you pry around?"

The next morning, we packed up again and headed for downtown. The back of the car was a mess of empty water bottles, candy wrappers, and half-put-away camping gear. We had breakfast and went to find a bunch of flowers for my grandmother. Cadence found an antique store, where she bought a gift for her boyfriend. I was tempted to buy a stuffed animal for my grandmother, but that seemed kind of a risky gift for an eighty-five-year-old woman. We had a map of Eugene and I had the street address of my grandmother that I had copied off a rejection letter of my father's from 1956. In the old days of writing, people actually took the time to drop you a line when they rejected you. I have a strange little pile of rejection postcards and letters of my father's. In those days, there were typos and strange cryptic handwriting, telling my father they didn't want his poems or did want them.

My grandmother's house was in a seedy part of town. Her house was not old and quaint but sad and decrepit. We parked in front and walked around the surprisingly sturdy metal fence that surrounded the falling-down house. I could see evidence of a garden in the back. I tried to match it up with the photo that my father had burned fourteen years ago of my grandmother in Capri pants, a cigarette in her hand, sitting in a garden. Cadence was willing to brave the barking dog and go up to the back door and knock. I wasn't willing to risk her getting bitten by this unknown dog. Finally we knocked on the door of a neighboring house and found out that this wasn't the right house. Apparently my father had either lived here for a while or had used this house as a temporary mailing address after he had gotten out of the mental institution. My grandmother had never lived there.

"Well, that's a relief," Cadence said.

I felt almost giddy. I hadn't wanted my grandmother to live in this house. The only problem was that I didn't know where to go next. For years my grandmother had chosen to have her phone number and address unlisted to keep reporters from coming to her door. I tried her number again and there was no answer. "Let's go to the library and see if they have old phone books. She had to have her address listed at some point in history," I told Cadence.

No one that we talked to at the library had heard of my father—I found this strangely ironic—but they did send us in the direction of the old city directories, which at one time had the name, address, and occupation of everyone in Eugene. I sorted through the stacks of directories and found my grandmother's address and my stepgrandfather's occupation. He had worked at Wyatt's Tire shop.

My grandmother's house was only a couple of miles from the library. The library was built in the 1960s, so I knew that my father had never been there. We passed by a Wyatt's Tire, which is a chain, and I wondered if it was the same tire shop that my stepgrandfather had worked at. My father told me he had had a variety of stepfathers, all of them mean, except his last one. The one who worked at the tire shop. He was a good man. Taught my father to hunt, and liked to go fishing, and on my father's thirteenth birthday bought him his first gun.

My grandmother lives in a rural-looking neighborhood, not fancy but by no means poor. A lower-middle ground of income. My breathing became shallow as we turned down her street and started following the house numbers to hers.

*My grandmother's house
in Eugene, Oregon, 1961.*

We parked across the street from a small, neat, faded white house in the middle of a huge lot of recently cut grass. To the left of the house I could see the willow tree from the photo my father had destroyed so many years before. It stood next to an old clothesline, some pretty flowers, and, of course, blackberry bushes.

Cadence looked at me. "Do you want me to go with you?" I shook my head. Cadence sat down on the grass near where we had parked. I turned and looked back at her one last time. She gave me an encouraging wave and looked serious, squinting into the sun.

I kept walking. Cadence told me later that what she was wishing at that point was that Mary Lou would feel the healing power of love and open the door. "Please open the door, Mary Lou. Please open the goddamn door and let her in."

My grandmother's front door had a large pane of glass in it, and there were two tiny windows on either side of the door, all with the curtains shut tight. I knocked hard enough so that she could hear me. I had been practicing this knock for two years in my mind. There was silence. I looked around the porch. There were many blooming petunias that had been recently watered and a bag of potting soil. It was becoming hotter. Sweat dripped down my nose and the flowers felt awkward in my arms. I heard a little noise from within and a truly miraculous thing happened. The door opened a crack.

Part 2: A pretty good hamburger

"Who is it?" came a slightly raspy yet unwavering voice.

"Your granddaughter Ianthe, your son Richard's daughter. Can I talk to you?"

"Well, first I have to get some underwear on."

"Okay."

She shut the door.

I turned and waved at Cadence, who had stopped squinting and stood up.

The door opened and my grandmother, a tiny figure, looked up at me, and then gestured for me to follow. I walked into the sweet pungent smell of an elderly person's home. She was bowed over, and she winced as she sat down across from me in a chair in a small yellow kitchen.

"Well," she said tartly. "I thought you'd have two heads and a forked tongue."

"Why?" I burst out, astonished, still holding the flowers I had brought for her.

"I just did."

I looked around for a vase to put the flowers in. She directed me towards a vase and then I stood in the middle of the kitchen, not knowing what to do with them. "Put them on the stove," she said. So I did and then I sat down on a kitchen chair and dug through my bag nervously for the book of my father's that I had brought for her.

"I have a present for you," I said. It was the last compendium that Houghton Mifflin had published with the cover of *The Abortion*. When I handed it to her, Mary Lou took the book in her small hands and held the cover up close and stared intently at the black-and-white photo of my father. My father is thirty-five years old in the picture. She had not seen her son since he was twenty-one years old.

Suddenly she began to cry. Deep racking sobs shook her entire body. I put my hand on her shoulder.

And then she looked up and said, "I don't know you, do I?"

"I don't know you either," I replied, looking around for some Kleenex.

The kitchen was dim. The curtains were drawn, perhaps to keep the temperature down in the house. The kitchen seemed frozen in time. All the appliances were yellow and looked brand-new. I was startled when I realized that they were the same color that my father had chosen for his kitchen in Montana.

Her eyes were bright and she spoke without hesitation. Her hair was curly and white, capping her face in an almost mischievous manner. I reached into my bag again and pulled out a pen and paper and placed my camera on the floor. I had questions about my history and my father. And she began answering them as quickly as I could ask them. After Prohibition ended, "Moonshine Bess," as my great-grandmother was called by some people, bought a tavern down in St. Helens. "Bessie left us kids up in Tacoma and sent us money every month. You see, my mother was a business woman," Mary Lou said.

"Did my dad have a paper route?" My father had told me that

when he was young he had a paper route in order to pay for his school clothes.

"Richard picked beans all one summer to buy an old broken-down bike so that he could have a paper route. They had stopped making bikes during the war, so they were expensive. He paid fifty dollars for that bike and it wasn't worth even five dollars. He picked string beans every summer until he was old enough to work in the cannery, and then he worked there every season until he was out of high school. He did all sorts of odd jobs to make money."

"Did he ever get a brand-new bike?"

"No."

Floods of facts poured so fast from her tiny body that finally I gave up trying to write things down and asked her if she minded if I taped her.

"You must be rich," she said.

"Why would you say that?"

"Because of the tape recorder and the camera."

"The tape recorder and the camera are borrowed. I'm not poor, but I'm far from rich," I answered.

I glanced hungrily around. There was a dining-room table with some stacks of papers and a living room which I couldn't see into all that well. I hoped that she would show me around later. I sat back down again, sure that by the time Cadence checked on me, Mary Lou and I would be about done talking. This was not to be the case.

Cadence appeared almost instantly, it seemed, although an hour had passed. Mary Lou took to my "little friend," and Cadence persuaded Mary Lou to let her take a picture of the two of us. Mary Lou thought she had a giant nose and didn't like to have her picture taken. "I'm not photogenic, you know."

I knelt on the floor beside her and we both smiled at Cadence. "Drop dead, Ianthe," Mary Lou joked under her breath, and then she waved at the video camera and said in a nice great-grandmotherly voice, "Hello, Lizzie. I'm your great-grandmother."

After Cadence put the camera away she perched on a little stool by the sink. That sink had an incredible attraction for me. My father had washed many dishes at that sink. The house was so small I was not even sure how my tall father fit into it. I couldn't believe that this tiny woman was my grandmother. And I told her so.

"Well, your great-great-grandmother Madora Sonora Ashlock was six feet three inches tall."

"Really."

Mary Lou was so sharp that she didn't get confused or lost.

My grandmother, Mary Lou, and me, in Eugene, Oregon, 1995. © Paul Swensen

She just jumped the tracks of memory to the next question I had. And I soon realized that she had some things she wanted me to know.

"Richard used to trade his nice clothes to the twins down the road."

I can't quite imagine this, but what do I know?

And then Mary Lou abruptly changed the subject. "He never beat you or anything?"

"Never. Never. He never beat me," I said.

"Did he give you lots of loving?"

"He gave me a lot. He loved me very much."

I didn't say anything for a moment. She looked at me a little concerned. "After Richard was born I had to go to work. I hated to leave him. I left him with a German lady. I cried every day." Her voice lowered. "He got sick, and when I took him to the doctor, they said he was malnourished." Her voice got even lower. "The lady wasn't feeding him." I wanted to cry, because I could see my father walking around in dirty diapers, hungry. I wanted to ask her more but her face looked fragile as a cobweb. I hadn't come here to hurt her. There had been enough of that. There was no retribution to be paid.

Mary Lou wouldn't even let me get close to asking where his father was. Instead she started talking about her brother Edward's death during the war. My father had told me about his Uncle Edward. He had died in Sitka, Alaska, while working as an engineer in the army during World War II. Mary Lou and Edward had been a team. It was him that she came home to when she found herself pregnant and alone in 1935. "You see, it was the Depression, hon." The way that Mary Lou pronounced the word "Depression" was odd. I had never heard the word said that way before. She dug in on the first syllable, and then pressed her lips firmly together on the second, leaving the last syllable to drift away. "There wasn't any money and there wasn't any work."

Tacoma was where my father lived for the first eight years of his life. They were poor. Yet, there is a studio photograph of my father on a tricycle. My Aunt Barbara said she never remembered any tricycle. My father had fond memories of Bessie. She gave him a sailor suit.

Mary Lou's memory of dates made my mind reel. She remembered when my father was baptized, when her stepfather died, when she was married and when her mother died, when her grandmother died, and even the names of the undertakers. "Richard had an excellent memory, you know." I nodded my head and wanted to add, So does his mother. Births, baptisms, and deaths.

"Your father was baptized Catholic," she told me and then recited everyone who attended. My dad's father, Bernard Brautigan, was an enigmatic figure. My father said he had met him only twice. When he was about four, Mary Lou had pushed him into a room with his father. My father watched him shave without saying a word and then his father handed him a dollar. And the second time my father was about six or seven and passed him on a street near the restaurant where his mother was working as a cashier. His father stopped and said hello and gave him fifty cents.

"What were the Brautigans like?"

"Those Brautigans," she burst out. "Always killing themselves. One sister killed herself, and a brother did too." Mary Lou said she had married Bernard Brautigan when she was sixteen. This had upset her mother, Bessie. I knew that Bernard Brautigan had denied that my father was his child.

My father, around 1939.
Permission of Barbara
Fitzhugh

"Why didn't he want to admit that he was my dad's father?"

"Brautigan was Catholic. The woman he was with wanted to get married in the church, and he couldn't do that if he had been married to me." My Aunt Barbara had told me that Mary Lou told my father that his last name was Brautigan just before he graduated from high school. Mary Lou thought his diploma should have "the correct name." Up to that point in my father's life, he had thought his last name was Portersfield. For some reason I believed Mary Lou. She had no reason to lie about this.

"Was your mother a nice person?" I asked.

"Oh, yes, she was very well liked," Mary Lou answered promptly.

"Did she have a temper?" I didn't know about the rest of the family, but my father had a temper.

Mary Lou nodded her head vigorously. "You should have heard her yelling at her help in the tavern."

"Do you believe in God?" I asked her suddenly.

She looked at me impatiently. "Why should I? What did God ever give me but grief?"

Did you get invited over to play if your mother had been divorced and made a living as a bootlegger? How did Bessie explain this to her? Did Bessie care? Mary Lou didn't seem to. My father didn't. In an odd way, I could see that his family background had given him the kind of outsider view that one needs in order to be an artist. And I could see that his quick wit had originated from Mary Lou.

"How many times have you been married?" she asked me.

"Only once," I replied. "Do you think it's a good idea to be married?"

"Heavens no," she said.

"Why?"

"Men can be trouble."

She broke the mood. "Richard was real smart, read all the time. Always had a paperback in his pocket."

"What did he read?"

"You know, those *Reader's Digests*. And he was always helping the other boys with their schoolwork. He had the nicest friends. Good boys."

"If he was so good in school how come he didn't go to college?"

My grandmother leaned forward and held out her empty hands. "There was no money for that sort of thing. Papa would come home and give me his paycheck and we'd sit at the kitchen table and pay the bills, and he gave me what little was left. I'd say, 'No, keep some for yourself,' and he'd say, 'No, you keep it.'"

"He was a good man, wasn't he?"

My father in his junior year in high school.
Permission of
Barbara Fitzhugh

She nodded her head, "Papa was half American Indian. I wish he hadn't up and died on me. He took your father hunting all the time. We ate like royalty, eating pheasant and the like."

My father had stopped hunting by the time I was born. Occasionally he had gone with Jim Harrison and Tom McGuane, but I never got the impression that he cared much for it. Still, I had no idea how much time he'd spent hunting as a teenager.

"Richard fished so much that he kept everybody in the neighborhood in fish."

"Did he fish when he was younger?" I asked.

"He used to go over to the Mill Pond and catch catfish when he was about ten. I wouldn't eat them because they had whiskers, but Richard would skin them and dip them in batter and fry them up."

"So he knew how to cook?"

"Oh, yeah. That kid loved corn on the cob."

While I was trying to think of something else she leaned forward.

"Do you know why he killed himself?"

"I don't know," I answered. There was a silence. The day had slipped away.

Cadence stood up and stretched. "Do you mind if I walk around?"

"There are some pictures on the dining-room table," Mary Lou said. She got up gingerly and walked bent-over to the dining room. I stepped ahead of her, then turned to ask her if I could go into the darkened living room.

"Sure, honey," she said. Her living room was overflowing with stuffed animals. Teddy bears of all sorts of sizes and shapes sat perched on all the available surfaces. My impulse to buy her a stuffed animal instead of flowers had been correct.

"I didn't know you liked stuffed animals."

"I didn't know either until somebody gave me one," was her curt reply, and then she came up behind me and picked up one fluffy white bear and brushed off the top of its head. "The dust, you know. That's the problem with getting old. You can't dust very well. Give this to Lizzie."

Together we found a paper bag to ensure the bear's safe journey home. I asked her to write a little note to my daughter to go with the bear. "For Lizzie, from your great-grandmother Mary Lou."

Once again seated in the kitchen, we went through a stack of old black-and-white photos. A beautifully dressed doll sitting on a couch. Flowers. "I had quite a garden back then. I'd work in the garden all day and then have a beer or two. Nothing wrong with that, is there?"

It was my turn to shrug my shoulders.

"Is there anything you would really like to do?" I asked her.

She raised a hand and fluttered it in front of her. "Fly."

"Where?" I imagined exotic choices like France.

"Around here."

"Why?"

"I would just like to look down on everything," she said, before handing me a picture of her yard in the sixties.

It was beautiful. We both liked nasturtiums and pansies. She gave me a picture of her in a new winter coat thirty-five years ago. She was hugging the coat with pleasure. I asked for a picture of her yard in its glory days, when she was still able to spend hours outside. And she gave me a duplicate of the picture my father had burned. Mary Lou and Papa, my step-grandfather, sitting under the willow tree in the backyard. I held the photo carefully. My father had hidden this aspect of his family. He had always told me we were white trash. He was wrong. The little house I had been sitting in for seven hours showed evidence of people who worked hard to make what they had better.

Mary Lou told me that the living room had been added on after my father left, but his bedroom was built when he was in high school. So this was the room he started writing in. I peeked into it, now a storage room. The door was closed and the window was covered with an old-fashioned venetian blind. My Aunt Barbara inherited this room after he left. There wasn't any heat and the winters were cold. My Aunt Barbara told me he used to sit and type, even on the cold nights. Before this room was built he slept on the davenport in the living room. And before that, poverty. Mary Lou alone in the Depression. Mary Lou and the drunken dangerous stepfathers. My Aunt

Barbara told me that she and my dad would walk for miles along the side of highways with an old baby buggy collecting glass returnables to make much-needed money in the winter. I knew that a son could be so overwhelmed by the past that he spent time in a mental institution at the age of twenty-one.

"Why did my dad go to the mental institution?"

"It was a court-ordered evaluation. He stayed up in there for thirty or sixty days."

"Why did the court do that?"

"He went to the police station and said, 'Arrest me.' They said, 'We have no reason to arrest you.' So Richard went outside and threw a rock at their window and said, 'Now you do.' We drove up there once a week to see him." What did those psychiatrists think, anyway, of this smart-mouthed mother, and hard-working Native American stepfather who in no way resembled the tall, ethereal young man, my father?

The last question I asked Mary Lou was if she ever had dreams for her life. She pretended not to understand the question. "There was no time for dreaming. In those days it took everything a person could do just to get a meal at the end of the day. By the time I laid my head on the pillow, I was so tired I could only sleep. There was no dreaming."

The sun began to set. I wanted to take her out to dinner, but she thought it would be too expensive for me. "Besides, air-conditioning bothers me. Why don't we just order some burgers and eat them here." She picked up the phone and called the local burger place and made our order. After she had completed the order she said sharply, "And hurry it up." I raised my eyebrows at her and she giggled.

Mary Lou then got up to get up her purse. "No, no, Mary

Lou. This is my treat," I said. "After all, how many times do I get to buy dinner for my grandmother?"

Mary Lou kept moving for her purse. "You kids are not made of money," she said firmly.

"It's Ianthe's treat," Cadence said.

Mary Lou became very concerned. "But you may have an accident driving and you'll need money."

"No, we have credit cards," I reassured her.

"Do you have credit cards?" Mary Lou double-checked.

"We have credit cards and money. We've got everything," I repeated.

"Well, one of us has credit cards," Cadence said.

"Cadence lost her wallet at Limberlost campground," I explained.

Mary Lou stopped reaching for her purse and looked at Cadence. "What driver's license are you driving on now?"

Cadence hung her head in mock shame and said, "Nothing. I'm bad, very bad."

We all burst out laughing. Mary Lou and I both had the same kind of booming laugh.

"You'll have to quit telling me all this bad stuff," Mary Lou said, and we laughed even harder. And then Mary Lou gave Cadence precise instructions to the burger place and suddenly added, "Now, be careful, don't get lost." And then she turned back to me and put her hand on my shoulder. "I just met you. I don't want to lose you."

Cadence went off to get the burgers and shakes, while Mary Lou and I set the table. When Cadence got back, we transferred the burgers onto plates, and Mary Lou passed me a pile of napkins.

"How did you know I like lots of napkins?" I asked.

"Well, you're my granddaughter, aren't you?"

There was no talk for a while. It had been a long, hot day and we were all hungry. Mary Lou finally broke the silence. "This is a pretty good hamburger, don't you think?"

All That Is Left Are Dragons

Well, I'm almost done," I told my family at the dinner table.

"What are you writing this time?" my daughter asked.

"The book about your Grandpa Richard."

She took a bite of salad and smacked thoughtfully. I gave her the look. She closed her lips and swallowed and then made flying gestures with her fork. "Why don't you put some dragons in your book?"

I looked puzzled.

She reassured me, "Oh, your dad could still be in it, but there could be riding dragons too."

Elizabeth loved dragons. The dragons she draws are mythical, magical, wise, witty, and at times scary, like her grandfather.

After dinner, she and I went back to work. She was building a miniature medieval village. The knights had tinfoil armor. Elizabeth has discovered that old balloons can be cut up to make authentic-looking leather capes. She has used some sheets of my printer paper to cut and color in the shape of a river, which flows through her little town.

We both woke up early the next morning, and worked in tandem. She uses a little pantry next to my office for a playroom. Paul and I let her paint the walls as a backdrop for her village. There is a dark blue sky and rolling hills and lots of trees.

When I looked over her shoulder, a complicated village was taking shape. I could see a feast, complete with a little plastic fish and pig on a platter alongside side dishes of Play-Doh food. Her livestock was eating binder paper cut in strips to look like hay. The green dragon lived on an island with a sorcerer, surrounded by a moat. Elizabeth was in the process of putting her townsfolk to sleep. She didn't look up but murmured, "Trying to find a bed for everybody is hard."

Birthday

This morning in the early hours of my birthday I received a gift. My father invited me to come visit in a dream. In this one, he was living in a new apartment near Geary Street in San Francisco. The interiors looked like a sunnier version of his Geary Street apartment, but in the dream we spent most of our time in his backyard. My father had taken up gardening. He had prepared several raised flower beds.

"I need more space," he complained to me.

I hugged him and told him he was lucky to have the view and the amount of space that he did have. And he was. His backyard looked out into endless rolling golden hills. He took me to the middle of Golden Gate Park to a smaller version of the Palace of Fine Arts tucked in the middle of a dark leafy grove of trees. There were lots of poets wearing corduroy jackets with drooping satin linings milling about the stone floors, waiting. Lew Welch and my father gave a poetry reading. I stood leaning against a white marble pillar near the front. After the reading I found some lettuce plants to give to my father for his new garden, with the instructions "They need to be watered." I went back to my father's apartment and gave him the housewarming gift.

In the dream, I worried about my father, just as I had in life. Did he have everything he needed? I sat in his sunny front room and wondered if I should give him my VCR, but then I noticed he had one. I went back to the poetry palace. Now it was empty except for me. I wandered around this extraordinary place alone. This is where most of my dreams about my father end. My being left alone again. But in this dream something changed. He had a home. I could go visit him. And so I did, and we stood in his

My father and me in Washington Square Park, San Francisco, 1962.
© Virginia Aste

kitchen together. The morning air was singing through the apartment. His hair was unbrushed and he was wearing a white T-shirt. I was wearing shorts and a T-shirt. Both of us were holding cups of instant coffee. He looked at me and said, "You know, I would really like it if Elizabeth could come down and visit me. She could spend the night." A surprising joy crept through me. I remembered all the good mornings and days I had spent with my father, and I was deeply grateful he wanted to share that with Elizabeth.

"That would be really nice," I said and we stood there bathed in the seemingly endless sunlight that filled this new home of his until I woke up.

Later on that day I cried because it made me sad to realize how much Elizabeth and my father missed in not meeting each other. He would have loved going to her basketball games and bragging about her intelligence. But some things are not meant to be. I was glad that my father finally had a safe place to live. Being an enormous, magical father, he will always want more space.

I'm glad I had the courage to wander alone with sharp objects tempting the release of a pain that has resided in me for so long. I have found that from my walking in painful places long enough, the knife edges, formerly so sharp, become dull. All they are good for, in the end, is to spread butter on toast for breakfast I will eat with my child. My flesh is safe. My father is safe. My words are safe in this pale new dawn that I share with my father.

> "Where did that kid go, Mother?"
> "I don't know, Father.". . .
> "I don't see him anywhere."
> "I guess he's gone."
> "Maybe he went home."
>
> —R.B., So the Wind Won't
> Blow It All Away